HEART
Eat Your Heart Out with Morro & Jasp

Library and Archives Canada Cataloguing in Publication

Morro and Jasp (Performing group), author--
    Eat your heart out with Morro and Jasp / Morro and Jasp.

ISBN 978-1-926639-72-7 (pbk.)

    1. Cooking. 2. Cooking--Humor. 3. Cookbooks. I. Title.

TX714.M677 2013   641.5   C2013-905703-X

Copyright 2013 Unit Productions Inc.
All rights reserved

Illustrations: Heather Marie Annis
Editors: Amy Lee and Byron Laviolette
Photography: Alex Nirta
Cover Design: Lisa Plekhanova
Copyeditor: Myna Wallin

Tightrope Books Inc.
167 Browning Trail
Barrie, Ontario
L4N 5E7

Printed in Canada at Coach House Printing

We thank the Canada Council for the Arts and The Ontario Arts Council for their support of our publishing program

Welcome

WARNING

~ No clowns were harmed in the making of this cookbook, although it does contain the blood, sweat and tears of two clown sisters.

~ Any resemblance to any characters or recipes that are already out there in the ether is a total coincidence. So don't sue us. Please.

Foreword

by Amy Pataki

We all eat our feelings.

A professional food taster like me is no different. Sure, I rate restaurants for the Toronto Star, a pinch-me-I'm-dreaming job that on any given night could mean feasts of Kobe beef, lobster tails or foie gras.

But on an emotionally taxing day, all I want is plain buttered pasta.

This happens frequently. I go home and make a big pile of linguine, then consume every last slippery strand in a ritual I enjoy almost as much as the simplicity of what I'm eating. I twirl it up from the same blue-and-white Chinese porcelain bowl on the same spot on the couch, with the same seasoning of flaked Maldon sea salt, cracked pepper and freshly grated parmesan. Each bite is intensely comforting.

Emotion drives eating. There's a reason why so many restaurants have adopted the comfort-food trend in North America: It sells.

People love ordering dishes like "mom's meatloaf" with mashed potatoes, even if it tastes nothing like their mother's. In fact, their mother could be a terrible home cook who boils steak and whose jello salad everyone avoids at potlucks ever since nice old Mr. Sheldon inadvertently bit into a bottle cap. Yet such foods promise a return to childhood and its seemingly simpler problems. (To trivialize those difficulties is wrong. A 9-year-old girl's social ostracization is as real to her as Mr. Sheldon's need for a new crown.)

Then there are the foods that fuel our anger, drown our sorrow and assuage our disappointment. And they are collected in Eat Your Heart Out with Morro and Jasp, an emotionally driven clown cookbook that matches feelings to recipes.

Morro and Jasp are comic originals whose show Morro and Jasp: Go Bake Yourself sends up our fascination with Food Network programming.

The show, in case you haven't seen it, is funny. There's Jasp, with her tightly wound hair and even more tightly wound persona, quoting Virginia Woolf and trying to control the messy and loud Morro during the taping of a faux cooking show. Picture a battle between super ego and id in clown form, with a bit of Julia Child thrown in – if Julia Child ever strove to make a love potion. Yet their feelings of excitement, sadness and hope seem real.

Turns out the recipes are, too. Okay, maybe not the "Super Sexy Seductive Soufflé" – a misguided love potion foisted onto volunteer audience members -- but these clowns can cook. They've divided recipes into chapters like Heartbroken, Nostalgic and Romantical – a concept much more helpful than by course. Take that, Mario Batali.

So next time I'm feeling blue, I might turn to "Drunken Mushroom Stew" instead of my usual bowl of linguine.

Speaking of which, the movie Ratatouille said "anyone can cook." Let's take it further: Everyone should eat – and laugh.

Amy Pataki is the restaurant critic for the Toronto Star.

Introduction

Ladies and Gentlemen, Boys and Girls, Creatures of the Universe,

We are Morro and Jasp. We are sisters, clowns, chefs, kooky inventors, writers, artists, players, lovers, fighters and friends, and we are so happy you could join us here – in our book.

The idea for this book sprouted when we began hosting our very own cooking show – Morro and Jasp: Go Bake Yourself. We performed it a whole bunch of times, like 127 or something, and we discovered that while we all love to eat, we often eat for different reasons at different times. In some cases, we eat because we're happy, and sometimes we eat because we're sad, and sometimes we even eat because we're just plain bored. If you've ever felt this way, then this book is for you.

What lies ahead is a collection of recipes to help you find the foods that suit your moods. Like when you want to impress a loved one, or when you want to enjoy that old favourite that makes you feel like you're a kid again, or when you want an energy boost to help you seize the day. Regardless of what you're feeling, we know you'll find a delicious recipe that will meet you on your own level; something you can be proud of making, sharing and eating.

In order to create this mouthwateringly delicious collection, we reached out to friends, family and fans. As a result, we got to hear so many stories and try so many new foods, each with their own twist or special memory. As soon as we asked people what they loved to cook, it opened up a whole world of exciting opinions and thoughts and, best of all, feelings – good, bad and everything in between.

We also learned through this process that not everyone likes to eat the same thing, or is able to eat all the things that others can, so we've tried our darndest to provide you with a range of dishes for any palate or diet. Almost all of the recipes in this book use ingredients that you should be able to find pretty easily. There are a couple that might be a little trickier to find, but just think of the adventures you'll have tracking them down. It will be fun! Trust us.

Finally, we want you to feel free to play with, in, and on top of your food. These pages should be the start of an exciting journey, not a rule book. If you like more of one thing or less of something else, then follow your heart and see what you come up with. This might be easier with some recipes than others (like the baked goods) but how you use this cookbook is totally up to you.

This book is also filled with drawings, poems, stories, letters and helpful hints. Whenever we put on plays, we love it when the audience plays along with us, and so we wanted to do the same thing in here. Since we can't actually be with you while you're cooking (although that would be fun), we want you to know that we're always there in spirit (like fairies though, not like ghosts...that would be bad...unless it's a friendly ghost...or a friendly ghost fairy) and we would love for you to share your cooking adventure stories with us, be it through the written word, online, or even just telepathically...

So off you go! We hope you have as much fun playing with this book as we had making it. And if you're ever feeling lonely, open this book and make something. It might help you feel less alone (if you want to, that is). If we've learned anything, it's that cooking is about love, sharing and togetherness. Food brings people together. You'll see.

Much love and eat your heart out!

XO MORRO & Jasp

About the Authors

MORRO

Jasp ♡

we look so serious.

I think I look pretty good.

us in real life

us in cartoon life

Morro thinks that people think too much. They should get out there and get messy. That's why she loves cooking. It always ends up in a huge mess - unless Jasp is raining on her parade. Morro is the younger sister and tries to remind Jasp that she needs to loosen up more. In terms of food, Morro is a vegimatarian who doesn't eat the meats, but she doesn't judge people who do. It's just not for her. She LOOOOOVES fresh foods, especially when they are local and in season - like apples and peaches and tomatoes and carrots. She also makes a mean pie. She has been called a tomboy before, but is not sure she is one. She likes sports (soccer-baseball is her fave) but is also okay being soft and gentle - but only when she feels like it. In short, Morro is really happy you're here and hopes you enjoy the foods and her drawings. She's proud of them. She wouldn't be insulted if you felt like drawing moustaches on them.

Jasp is a chef extraordinaire who has spent over 1000 minutes in the kitchen. She is not only a self-professed "foodie" but a culinary wizard who makes delicious things that usually involve cheese or dip, or a cheese dip of some kind. She is a complex creature who understands that life is about making a good impression and that love is never easy but totally worth it. Or so she hears. She hasn't found her "Mr. Right" yet but that's not because there is anything wrong with her. She's just picky. Her relationship with Morro is challenging at times, but only because her younger sister has so much still to learn. Jasp is patient with her, though, because it's the older sister's job to help the long lost lambs of this world (and Morro is more lost than most). In conclusion, you are lucky that she spent time making this cookbook. She worked really hard on the editing and she thinks you should know it. Now go, be bold, be beautiful, and one day maybe you'll be as good as her.

Table of Contents

Helpful Hinters.............................. 14

Playful... 21

Healthyful..................................... 37

Brave.. 55

Romantical................................... 77

Heartbroken.................................. 95

Angry... 109

I Need a Snuggle............................ 113

Lazy Dayzy.................................... 131

Nostalgic....................................... 147

Festive.. 165

Social... 181

Full of Love.................................... 197

Index.. 209

Helpful Hinters

So, we made a book. Which was magical, scary and took a lot of time. But in order to make the book, we had to make a whole bunch of food to figure out what recipes were awesome enough to make the cut. And while we made those recipes, we learned, like, a *lot* of things. Here are some of them:

1. Don't daydream. Well, okay, maybe a little bit as long as you stay focused. If you totally drift off into la-la land you will lose track of how many cups of water you put in, or how long the bread has been in the oven. Eyes on the prize, people.

2. Don't burn stuff. You can't take it back.

3. Read all of the ingredients. And the directions. And the labels on the ingredients. And do it carefully and with patience in your heart. Like, actually. If you don't, you might end up putting in 8 times more the amount of tomatoes in your Lamb Curry than you were supposed to, or using cornmeal to make your Maple Squash Pancakes instead of quinoa flour, rendering them inedible, or cooking your Raspberry Cupcakes at 275°F instead of 375°F, accidentally inventing the world's first ever slow roasted cupcake, which turned out to be not such a hit...you know, for example...

4. The "Toothpick Test" is your best friend when you're baking. In order to know if something is finished baking, poke a toothpick in the middle of it. If it comes out clean, you're good to go! If it comes out with goop on it, your dish ain't done! So put it back in and bake it a little bit longer.

5. When it says "in a double boiler," that doesn't mean you need to go out and buy a double boiler. You can boil a pot of water and put a heat proof bowl on top of it (we usually use a metal one), and put your ingredients in the bowl! Just make sure not to get water into the bowl.

6. When it says "divided," it means you're gonna use that ingredient for a couple of sections of the recipe – so don't throw it in all willy nilly.

7. When it says "olive oil," we usually recommend extra virgin olive oil. But if you're cooking with it at a higher heat, you have to be careful because olive oil has a lower smoke point. This means that when it heats up beyond 325°F -375°F, the oil can lose its wonderful healthiness and can actually become kinda bad for you. We learned that and thought you should know too...

8. A glug is of olive oil (Morro's favourite measurement) usually means one short-ish pour.

9. You can buy buttermilk if you really want to, but you can also make it yourself with stuff you probably have already. Put 1 Tbsp of vinegar or lemon juice in a liquid measuring cup. Then pour in milk until it reaches the 1 cup line. Wait 5 minutes and voila – buttermilk!

10. When we say "cream butter," it means make sure you mix it 'til it's light and fluffy and full of air. The air helps the baking rise.

11. Toasted nuts are delicious. Burnt ones, not so much. Toasting your nuts in the oven makes for much more even toasting. You can toast them in a pan, too, but make sure you watch them constantly.

12. Instead of table salt, you can crush up sea salt in a mortar and pestle. It's extra yummy that way. And better for you.

13. Don't over salt. You can always add more salt if you need it, but you can't take it away. If you eat something with too much salt, it will feel like the inside of your mouth is sucking up all the moisture that ever existed in your body. And that's just a gross feeling.

14. "Debearding" is to take off the byssal threads from the mussels (the fibers that are coming out of the shell), not shave someone's beard.

15. Don't be afraid to get messy. The stains you make in this book will be part of its story. And yours.

Hope that helps! Now go forth with confidence, grasshoppers!

Volume Conversion Chart

Imperial	Metric
1 teaspoon	5 mL
1 tablespoon *or* 1/2 fluid ounce	15 mL
1 fluid ounce *or* 1/8 cup	30 mL
1/4 cup *or* 2 fluid ounces	60 mL
1/3 cup	80 mL
1/2 cup *or* 4 fluid ounces	120 mL
2/3 cup	160 mL
3/4 cup *or* 6 fluid ounces	180 mL
1 cup *or* 8 fluid ounces *or* half a pint	240 mL
1 1/2 cups *or* 12 fluid ounces	350 mL
1 cup *or* 8 fluid ounces *or* half a pint	240 mL
1 1/2 cups *or* 12 fluid ounces	350 mL
2 cups *or* 1 pint *or* 16 fluid ounces	475 mL
3 cups *or* 1 1/2 pints	700 mL
4 cups *or* 2 pints *or* 1 quart	950 mL
4 quarts *or* 1 gallon	3.8 L

Note: If you don't have to be exactly exact, sometimes you can round up like this:
  1 cup = 250 mL
  1 pint = 500 mL
  1 quart = 1 L
  1 gallon = 4 L

← In case you don't know.

☆ make sure you fill the meniscus!

Imperial Cooking Conversion Chart

Unit:	Equals:	Also equals:
1 tsp.	1/6 fl. oz.	1/3 Tbsp.
1 Tbsp.	½ fl. oz.	3 tsp.
1/8 cup	1 fl. oz.	2 Tbsp.
¼ cup	2 fl. oz.	4 Tbsp.
1/3 cup	2¾ fl. oz.	¼ cup plus 4 tsp.
½ cup	4 fl. oz.	8 Tbsp.
1 cup	8 fl. oz.	½ pint
1 pint	16 fl. oz.	2 cups
1 quart	32 fl. oz.	2 pints
1 liter	34 fl. oz.	1 quart plus ¼ cup
1 gallon	128 fl. oz.	4 quarts

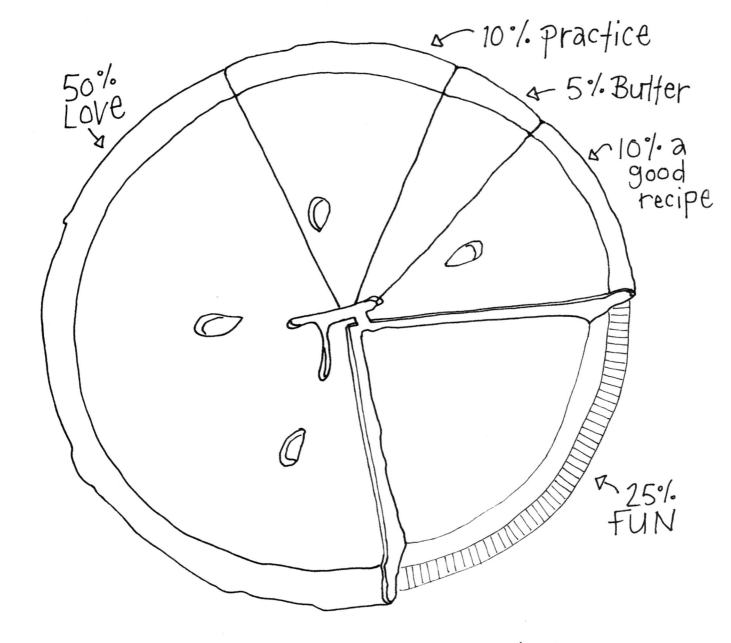

On the farm
It's so beautiful here. what is your name beautiful creature?
mmm beef brisket.
What kind of grain do you like best litte chicken?
mmmm... Chicken cordon bleu
get off me pig or you are going to be bacon so fast.
eeek. You are so cute I love you. You can come home with me and we'll be best friends
This carrot is awesome. I could live here FOREVER!
Ok seriously my allergies are really acting up. Let's go get some fastfood. mmm... Double bacon cheese Burger...

Are you ready to play with your food?

...Here come the recipies!

Playful

When you want the thrill of riding down a hill on your bike feeling the wind in your hair on a sunny day with your best friend and it's the start of summer vacation and you're going to get ice cream and they even have your fave flavour and then two hundred hummingbirds whisk you and your bestie away to a tropical island full of roller coasters and puppy dogs.

Wheeeeeeeeeeeeeeeee......!

Playdough...Yes Playdough!

Oatmeal Chocolate Chip Cookies

Hi Ho Ginger Pear Crumble

Peachy Keen Cobbler

Baloney Stew

Foo's Famous Krup-tooeys

Cookie Surprise

Na-Na-Naimo Bars

Super Awesome Frozen Ice Cream Peanut Butter Sponge Toffee Caramel Awesomeness

All the Cookies n' Ice Cream Cake

Summery Fresh Pasta

Morro & Jasp's Playtime Song

Play with me, friend
Don't say no
Play with me, friend
On adventures we'll go

To here! To there!
And back again.
On water, on land
So the fun never ends!

Let's wiggle and waggle
And shimmy and shake
And giggle and gaggle
'Til our tummies ache.

I can do it alone
But it's more fun with two
And there's nobody better
To play with than you!

So play with me, friend
Let's make a mess
Play with me, friend
Please say yes!

Playdough...Yes Playdough!
from Amelia and Elliot

1 cup flour
1 cup water
½ cup salt

2 Tbsp cream of tartar
1 Tbsp oil
food coloring (optional)

In a saucepan, mix all ingredients and cook over medium heat, continuing to stir until the mixture is stiff. Allow the mixture to cool and then knead thoroughly. Add food colouring to make it extra fun!

Store playdough in an airtight container in the fridge. Then play with it – that's what it's for.

This is NOT edible...Well you could eat it but it might not taste so good.

Use different colours to make a Rainbow!

Hi Morro! Hi Jasp!

My name is Emma and I have a recipe. It's not very special or different, but it's my favourite. My dad created the recipe and he taught it to me. We used to make cookies together when I was 4 (I learned how to make the perfect "lump" - which is what you call cookie dough when you're forming it into balls for the cookie sheet). I became the resident cookie maker in my house at age 8 - baking cookies for the family every week. Everyone had their own tin and would get to eat as many or as few cookies as they liked from their tin! But they wouldn't get any more until the next week when I made a new batch. It was a lot of responsibility - I'm sure you can imagine!

Now that I'm grown-up and still bake avidly I know that this isn't a particularly "special" recipe. But it is to me. I hope you love it.

Oatmeal Chocolate Chip Cookies

from Emma

4 cups quick oats
1/2 tsp salt
1/2 Tbsp baking soda
3/4 cup white sugar
3/4 cup brown sugar
3/4 cup whole wheat flour
1 tsp cinnamon

2 eggs
1/2 cup oil
1 tsp vanilla extract
1 – 1 1/2 cups chocolate chips
(depending on your chocolatey preference)

Preheat oven to 350°F

Mix together the dry ingredients. In another bowl, crack the eggs and blend with oil and vanilla extract. Pour the wet ingredients into the dry and mix with spatula. If the mixture is too crumbly, you can add in a splash of milk or an extra egg. Form into lumps. Bake for 8-12 minutes. Enjoy!

Hi Ho Ginger Pear Crumble
from Sheila

Some people may like this sweeter so you could add more sugar, but I like it not so sweet and served with ice cream.

6 medium sized pears, peeled and sliced
1 tsp brown sugar
2 Tbsp raw organic coconut oil
(it's nice when it's really warm out because the coconut oil has a high liquid point, so it's easier to mix.)
2 Tbsp brown sugar
1 cup oatmeal
½ cup organic coconut, shaved
(any nuts will do, chopped)
1 nob of fresh ginger root, grated
cinnamon

Preheat oven to 350°F

Mix pears with 1 tsp brown sugar and place in an oven safe dish.

In a large bowl, mix coconut oil with brown sugar. Add oatmeal, shaved coconut, nuts and ginger root and mix it all together. Pour the mixture on top of fruit and sprinkle a little cinnamon across the top.
Cover and bake for about 45 minutes.

Peachy Keen Cobbler
from Peachy Keen

6-8 fresh peaches, peeled and sliced (enough to cover at least 1" of the bottom of the pan you are cooking in – the more the merrier!)
¼ cup white sugar
½ cup brown sugar
½ cup walnuts
½ cup oats
½ cup multigrain flour
½ cup butter
sprinkle of nutmeg
double sprinkle of cinnamon

Preheat oven to 325°F

Mix the peaches and white sugar together and spread in a glass baking dish. Mix everything else together, blending in butter with your fingertips. Don't be afraid to get a bit dirty. Sprinkle this oat-tacular mixture on top of the fruit.
Bake for 40 minutes.

Or sub in other fruits like apples and cranberries.

that's our friend Peachy Keen.

Baloney Stew
from Morro

This recipe is inspired by a middle-aged fireman who likes to ride motorcycles.

3-5 tsp butter
1-2 lbs bologna, chunked
1 onion, chopped
2 garlic cloves

5 potatoes, sliced or chunked
5 Tbsp flour
5 cups broth or water
salt & pepper to taste

Fry the bologna or bolognie or baloney (depending on how you feel like spelling it) in a dab of butter until it starts to brown. Use medium to low heat so the butter doesn't burn. Release the chunks of bolognie into a bowl for some chill out time. Add the potatoes and onions and fry them for a few minutes in a few more dabs of butter until they start to soften. Add flour to the pan with another dab of butter and whisk. Now you have a roux! Cook it until it gets a little browned and add the bologna back into the party. Pour in the broth and stir until it thickens. Cook it all for about 20 minutes-ish or until it's all tender to your liking. Top with ketchup. Mush it all together and enjoy!!!

Guess what? Did you know that Balogna is also known as 'newfie steak.

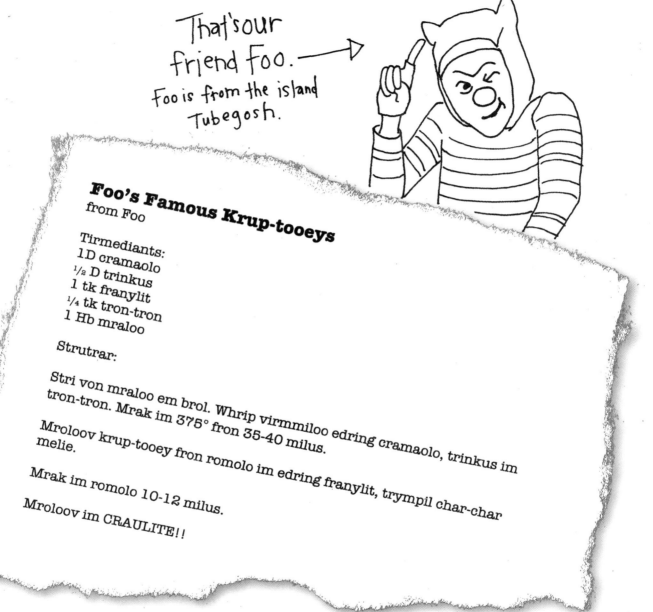

Cookie Surprise
from Caren

1 cup butter, softened
3/4 cup white sugar
3/4 cup brown sugar, packed
2 large eggs
1 tsp vanilla extract
2 1/2 cups flour

1 tsp baking soda
1/2 tsp salt
2 cups milk chocolate chips
4 caramel secret-filled chocolate bars, frozen (you know the ones)

Preheat oven to 375°F

Beat softened butter, sugars, eggs and vanilla in a large bowl. Mix together flour, baking soda and salt. Add the dry ingredients half at a time into the wet, and mix until blended. Stir in chocolate chips by hand and chill in the fridge for 10-15 minutes.

Remove chocolate bars from freezer and break into squares. Shape cookie dough over each chocolate square to cover and form into a small ball. Place on a greased cookie sheet and bake for 10 minutes or until lightly golden on top. When you take them out, press the cookie tops down with the back of a spoon so they are chewy and not cakey!

Variation: If you're a chocolate & peanut butter lover, you can use mini peanut butter cups instead of caramel chocolate squares!

Na-Na-Naimo Bars
from Morro

The Bastion
Nanaimo's
oldest 'ure

Crumb:
½ cup butter
¼ cup sugar
1 egg
4 Tbsp cocoa powder
2 cups graham wafer crumbs
1 cup coconut, shredded
½ cup walnuts, chopped

Filling:
½ cup butter
2 Tbsp milk
3 Tbsp vanilla custard powder or pudding powder
3 cups icing sugar, sifted

Topping:
4 squares semi-sweet cooking chocolate
1 tsp butter

To make the crumb, mix butter, sugar, egg and cocoa in a big bowl. Put it in a double boiler and stir it up until it looks like custard. If you don't know what custard looks like...well, you have led a misguided life, my friend.

Mix together graham wafer crumbs, coconut and nuts. Then mix that with the custard mixture, making sure they are nice and blended. Spread it into 8x8" pan and press down lightly – you don't want to hurt it, but you want it to stay put.

And now for the filling! Cream the butter, milk, custard powder and icing sugar. Slather it all over the bottom mixture in pan.

And finally, it's time to make the topping! Melt the chocolate in a double boiler then add butter and blend it nice and good. Spread it over the filling and let it set. Chill and keep in the fridge so it doesn't melt all over your hands when you go to eat it!

Super Awesome Frozen Ice Cream Peanut Butter Sponge Toffee Caramel Awesomeness
from Chef Eric

WoW!

Crust:
9 graham crackers, coarsely crushed
1/4 cup light brown sugar, packed
1/4 tsp kosher salt
1/8 teaspoon nutmeg, freshly grated
6 Tbsp butter, melted

Caramel Sauce:
1 cup brown sugar, packed
1/2 cup half-and-half
4 Tbsp butter
pinch of salt
1 Tbsp vanilla extract

Sponge Toffee:
1 cup sugar
1 cup corn syrup
1 Tbsp vinegar
1 Tbsp baking soda

Chocolate Sauce:
2 oz bittersweet chocolate
(do not exceed 61% cacao),
chopped
2 1/2 Tbsp unsalted butter

The Rest:
3 cups vanilla ice cream, slightly
softened
6 Tbsp smooth peanut butter
1/4 cup roasted peanuts

Preheat oven to 325°F

Finely grind graham crackers, sugar, salt, and nutmeg. Transfer crumb mixture to a medium bowl. Add butter and stir to blend. Use bottom and sides of a measuring cup to pack crumbs onto bottom and up the sides of 9" glass or metal pie pan. Bake until golden brown, about 15 minutes. Let cool, then freeze for 1 hour.

To make the caramel sauce, mix the brown sugar, half-and-half, butter and salt in a saucepan over medium-low heat. Cook while whisking gently for 5-7 minutes, until it gets thicker. Add the vanilla and cook another minute to thicken further. Turn off the heat, cool slightly and pour the sauce into a jar. Refrigerate until cold.

To make the sponge toffee, combine sugar, syrup and vinegar in a large saucepan. Stir over medium heat until sugar is dissolved. Continue to cook to 300°F (the hard crack stage). Remove from heat and stir in baking soda quickly – it will become frothy. Pour into a buttered pan. Cool and break into pieces.

To make the chocolate sauce, melt the chocolate and butter in a double boiler and whisk together.

Drizzle 1/2 cup caramel sauce over the bottom of the crust. Freeze for 30 minutes. Spoon ice cream into crust and smooth top. Freeze for another 30 minutes. Warm up 3 Tbsp of smooth peanut butter to drizzle over ice cream layer, and drizzle 2 Tbsp of chocolate sauce. Freeze for 2 hours. Pull the pie out of the freezer, place cracked sponge toffee over pie, drizzle more warm peanut butter and chocolate sauce over top. Garnish with roasted peanuts.

All the Cookies n' Ice Cream Cake
from Vania

60 of your favourite sandwich cookies, divided
¼ cup butter, melted
2 litres or 8½ cups ice cream, slightly softened

Note: You can use whatever kind of ice cream you want, but because of the sweetness of the cookies, you might just want to use something simple like vanilla.

To make the crust, crush 20 cookies. (Putting them in a sealable plastic bag and smashing with a rolling pin works well!) Mix the cookie crumbs with the melted butter. Layer it in the bottom of a springform pan and pat down flat.

For the filling, crush another 20 cookies. In a large bowl, stir the cookies into the ice cream. Pour this mix overtop of the crust.

For the topping, crush 20 more cookies and sprinkle over the top of the ice cream layer of the cake. Press the cookie bits down slightly so that they will stay put. (You can add anything else you want here, like caramel sauce or chocolate fudge.)

Cover the cake with plastic wrap and freeze for at least 3 hours or overnight to ensure the ice cream is good and solid.

♡ for easy cutting when serving. keep a tall glass of hot water beside the cake and dip the knife in between slices!

How to grow your dinner...

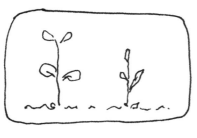

1. Plant a small plant of tomato and basil in good soil and in a place where they'll get lots of sun. (You can also grow them from seed — directions in our gardening book)

2. Water them every DAY!

3. Sing to them. Plants enjoy lots of music.

4. Encourage their growth by giving them pep talks every now and then.

5. Pick off the first round of yellow flowers on the tomato plant (even though they are pretty) so it'll get stronger before growing fruit.

6. Watch them grow! If there are slugs put some egg shells around the base of the plant.

7. Enjoy the fruits of your labour!

♡ MORRO.

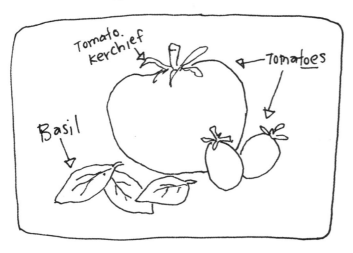

Summery Fresh Pasta
from Morro

This recipe only works with fresh grown tomatoes from the vine or from a farmers market because they have lots more flavour. Trust me, I know.

Sauce:
3-4 cups tomatoes (a mix of types is yummy and makes it pretty), chopped
sploosh of balsamic vinegar
a few glugs of olive oil
a couple handfuls of fresh basil, julienned
2-3 garlic cloves, crushed
parmesan, as much as you like
salt & pepper to taste

Chop your tomatoes and throw all the other ingredients into a bowl so they can party together and the flavours can mingle. Make your noodles (calm down - instructions below). Once the noodles are cooked, put them in a big bowl and pour your mixture of delicious tomatoes and basil on top. Sprinkle to your heart's content with fresh parmesan.

Pasta: *[noodles — don't you just love the word noodle]*
3 cups flour
3 eggs

Make a hill with the flour and then dig out a well in the middle. Break the eggs into the well so it looks like a volcano. With a fork begin to beat the eggs, slowly adding more and more flour until the eggs become dough. Be careful not to break the walls of the mound, or the volcano will overflow (if this happens just work the flour in fast). Keep mixing until you can knead the dough and until it is no longer sticky. It's alright if you haven't used all the flour.

Wrap it and let it rest for at least 20 minutes before you roll it out (it just went through a big transformation, okay?). Use a pasta roller or a rolling pin to roll and then cut slices by hand OR take off small pieces and roll into individual noodles (this might take a while). Good luck and good eating!

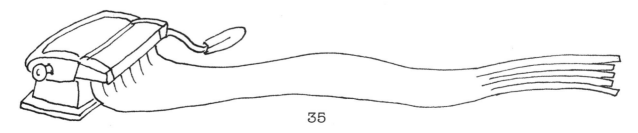

HEALTHYFUL

When you want to be good to your body and fill it with wholesome and nutritious things so that you've got the right stuff to get out there and make the most of the day. GO TEAM!

Keep fun and have fit.

Yummiest Brussels Sprouts

Yummiest Broccoli

Herb Garden Salmon

Chick Chicky Boom Chicken Salad

Avocado and Mushroom Super Salad

Kick Butt Kale Salad

Pump it Up Pear and Walnut Salad

Halloo-Me-Name Is-Raeli Couscous Salad

Fiesta Chickpea Salad

Fiesta Dressing

Overnight Layered Salad

Tickle My Tummy Tabbouleh Salad

I-Want-Junk-But-I'm-Watching-My-Figure Kale Chips

Sesame Lime Crunch Slaw

Homestyle Hummus & Pita Chips

Morro's Mean Lean Muffins

I Can't Believe They're Not Cookies

'What? I'm Eating My Veggies!' Zucchini Loaf

Eat Your Greens!

Yummiest Brussels Sprouts
from Morro

1½ lbs Brussels sprouts
¼ cup butter
3 shallots, finely chopped
½ cup fresh parmesan, shaved
1 tsp lemon peel, grated
salt & pepper to taste

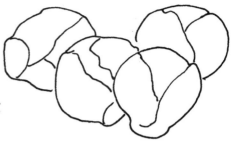

Even if you don't like Brussels sprouts you'll like these.

Cut off the hard Brussels sprout stems and chuck 'em in the compost. Then cut them into strips. In a big pot, boil some water and toss the sprouts in for 3-4 minutes, or until they're tender and bright bright green. Drain 'em good.

In a big pan, melt the butter at medium heat, then throw in the shallots and sauté until they start to get a little brown on the edges. Throw in the sprouts, parmesan and lemon zest. Mix it all up and add salt & pepper to taste – if you want.

Yummiest Broccoli
from Jasp

2 heads broccoli
2 Tbsp sesame oil
2 garlic cloves, crushed
2 Tbsp soy sauce
1 tsp white vinegar
salt & pepper to taste

Chop broccoli into small pieces and put them into a large pan or wok with enough water to cover the bottom of the pan. Cover with a lid and steam until bright green and tender.

Heat sesame oil in a large skillet over medium heat. Add garlic and sauté for 1 minute. Then add broccoli, soy sauce and vinegar. Stir and make sure broccoli is coated with everything. Add salt & pepper to taste.

You can use spinach, kale, or your favourite green veggies instead of broccoli and it's always yummy!

Herb Garden Salmon
from Michéle

1 large salmon fillet
2 Tbsp dill*
2 Tbsp chervil*
2 Tbsp basil*
1/2 cup fresh chives, finely chopped

2 bunches green onions, finely chopped
1 Tbsp Kosher salt
2 Tbsp canola oil
2 Tbsp lemon juice
2 garlic cloves, chopped

*Measurements based on dried herbs. For fresh herbs, double the amount.

Preheat oven to 400°F

Rinse salmon fillet and pat dry, then place on a foil-lined cookie sheet. Mix together herbs, salt, oil, lemon juice and garlic to create marinade. Rub marinade on top of the salmon fillet then flip over and rub the rest of the marinade on the bottom. Let marinate for 15 minutes. Flip the salmon fillet over again and rub the loose marinade from the bottom onto the top. Let marinate for another 15 minutes. Bake the salmon fillet for about 20 minutes.

Refreshing and Sweet!

* We boil our eggs for 15 minutes

Chick Chicky Boom Chicken Salad

from Don and Donna

2 cups cooked chicken, cubed
2 Tbsp lemon juice
1/2 tsp salt
1 cup celery, sliced
1 cup seedless green grapes, halved

1/4 cup mayonnaise
1/4 cup plain yogurt
2 hard boiled eggs, chopped
1/4 cup slivered almonds, toasted

Sprinkle the cooked chicken with lemon juice and salt and chill for several hours. Then add in celery, grapes, mayonnaise, yogurt and toss to blend. Add chopped eggs and almonds and toss lightly.

* We toast our almonds at 300°F for 10-15 minutes.

Hey those clowns are taking off with our food!

Avocado and Mushroom Super Salad
from Francie

4 Tbsp red wine vinegar
3/4 cup olive or canola oil
2 garlic cloves, chopped
2 Tbsp parsley flakes
1 1/2 tsp salt

1/2 tsp pepper
8 oz mushrooms, sliced
2 avocados, chopped
1/2 red onion, chopped

Mix together vinegar, oil, garlic, parsley, salt and pepper. Add mushrooms, avocados and red onion and make sure they are coated. Let mixture marinate for at least 30 minutes, then toss over romaine or red leaf lettuce.

✭ Be really careful if you decide to forage for mushrooms in the wild. There are a lot of poisonous ones so please consult an expert.

Kick Butt Kale Salad
from Kimwun

½ garlic clove, minced
¼ tsp kosher salt (plus a pinch)
¼ cup parmesan, grated (plus more to garnish)
3 Tbsp olive oil (plus more to garnish)
¼ cup lemon juice, freshly squeezed
⅛ tsp red chili flakes
pepper to taste
1 bunch kale, sliced into ribbons

Pound the garlic and salt together to form a paste. Then add parmesan, olive oil, lemon juice, pinch of salt, chili flakes, and pepper and whisk to combine.

Place the kale in a large bowl and pour the dressing over the kale and toss well, making sure all the kale is coated. Let the salad sit for 5 minutes, then serve topped with extra parmesan, and a drizzle of olive oil.

Pump it Up Pear and Walnut Salad
from Caren

4 fresh pears
⅓ cup lemon juice
3 Tbsp cider vinegar
2 Tbsp honey
1 Tbsp dijon mustard
⅛ tsp salt
¼ cup olive oil
1 head red leaf lettuce
¼ cup blue cheese, crumbled
¼ cup goat cheese, crumbled
¼ cup feta, crumbled
¾ cup walnuts, toasted
1 bunch green onions, diced
pepper to taste

Peel and slice pears and place in a bowl with lemon juice. To make the dressing, mix the vinegar, honey, dijon and salt in another bowl and whisk, adding in the oil slowly to emulsify the dressing. Tear the greens into pieces and place in a salad bowl, and add pears, cheeses, walnuts and green onions. Pour the dressing over top.

Halloo-Me-Name Is-Raeli Couscous Salad
from Ian

Dressing:
2 Tbsp Madras curry paste
1 garlic clove, minced
¼ cup fresh lime juice
2 Tbsp honey
½ cup olive oil

Salad:
½ cup Israeli couscous
3 cups cauliflower florets, halved (about ½ a head of cauliflower)
2 small Italian eggplants, cut into ½" slices
3 Tbsp vegetable or canola oil for brushing and grilling
1 block halloumi cheese, cut into 6 pieces
19 oz can chickpeas, drained and rinsed
½ cup dried apricots, quartered
2 cups baby spinach, rinsed and dried
2 Tbsp fresh parsley, chopped
salt to taste

Whisk dressing ingredients in a small mixing bowl and set aside.

Heat grill to medium-high or preheat the oven to 400°F

Toast the couscous grains by placing them in a saucepan on medium-high heat on the stove until they turn golden brown. Then cook the couscous according to the package instructions and set aside.

Brush cauliflower and eggplant with oil and grill until tender and lightly charred, about 6 to 8 minutes per side. Or roast the vegetables in the oven for 6 minutes on each side and then broil until slightly blackened. During the last 4 minutes, grill the halloumi for 2 minutes per side.

Once the cauliflower and eggplant are cool, coarsely chop them and place them in a large mixing bowl along with the couscous, chickpeas, apricots, spinach and dressing. Toss until well mixed. Stir in parsley and salt and place a piece of grilled halloumi overtop each serving.

Israeli couscous is usually made from wheat flour. It's also called pearl couscous, 'Jerusalem couscous' or 'ptitim'

Fiesta Chickpea Salad
from Jeni

1 can chickpeas, rinsed and drained
1 can black beans, rinsed and drained
1 can whole corn, rinsed and drained
1 small cucumber, sliced and quartered
1 cup cherry tomatoes, halved
1 small red onion, diced
1 avocado
a generous handful of cilantro
Fiesta Dressing (see below!)
1 cup shredded cheese (optional)

Combine chickpeas, black beans, corn, cucumber, tomatoes, and onion in a large bowl.
Drizzle dressing over and toss, adding in chopped cilantro. Finally, half the avocado, scoop out and cut into fairly small chunks then add to mixture.
Marinate the salad in the dressing for 20 minutes before serving.
For extra fun, you can add a sprinkling of your favourite cheese.

Fiesta Dressing
from Hannah

1/2 cup olive oil
1/2 cup red wine vinegar
2 Tbsp lime juice (1/2 a lime)
1 Tbsp lemon juice
2 Tbsp sugar
1 Tbsp salt
1 garlic clove, crushed
1/2 Tbsp cumin
1/2 Tbsp black pepper, ground
1 tsp cayenne pepper

Mix everything together. Bam!

We like it with this dressing. Yum! And Morro of course makes it with cilantro on the side so it can be optional

Overnight Layered Salad
from Lori

¾ cup mayonnaise
¾ cup sour cream
1 garlic clove, minced
½ cup parmesan, grated
1 Tbsp lemon juice
salt & pepper to taste
1 head romaine lettuce, chopped
2 tomatoes, chopped
½ bunch celery, chopped
1 red pepper, chopped
1 can water chestnuts, sliced
1 small package frozen peas, thawed
1 bunch green onions, chopped
2 hard boiled eggs, sliced
10 strips bacon, cooked and crumbled

For the dressing, mix together mayonnaise, sour cream, garlic, parmesan, lemon juice, and salt & pepper to taste.

In a large, clear glass bowl, layer in the following order: lettuce, tomato, celery, red pepper, water chestnuts, peas, dressing, and green onions. Pour mixture over the top of the salad and spread out evenly. Cover and refrigerate overnight. Garnish with bacon and hard boiled egg slices.

Tickle My Tummy Tabbouleh Salad
from Morro

All measurements and ingredients are optional – adjust to your taste buds or to suit what you have in your fridge. It's your own darn salad! Take some responsibility, people.

1 cup bulgur wheat or quinoa, cooked
1 red pepper, chopped
¼ cup mint leaves (optional, I don't always add them)
¼ cup green onions, diced
6 artichoke hearts, chopped (the kind from a jar)
2 medium sized tomatoes, sliced (or 1½ cups cherry or grape tomatoes, halved)
1 red onion, chopped fine (optional if you like lots of onion)
1 cucumber, chopped small
½ cup feta cheese, broken up or cut into small cubes – the smaller the better
sprinkle of cumin
dash of cayenne pepper
dash of balsamic vinegar
3 Tbsp olive oil
a few big squeezes of lime or lemon
generous handful of parsley (at least as much as the grain)
salt & pepper to taste

Isn't it self-explanatory? You chop the stuff up and toss it in a bowl – it's a salad.

I-Want-Junk-But-I'm-Watching-My-Figure Kale Chips
from Jasp

1 head of kale
1 Tbsp olive oil
1/4 tsp kosher salt
1 garlic clove, crushed

Preheat oven to 300°F

Wash and thoroughly dry kale and rip off chip-sized pieces from the big stem in the centre (don't include the stem in your chip mix – does it look like a chip to you?). Put the ripped kale in a large bowl and add the olive oil, salt, and garlic, and mix with your clean hands, to make sure all the leaves are coated. On 2 baking sheets, place the kale pieces in a single layer (very important). Bake for 5 minutes, check on them, then a few more minutes, then check on them again. They burn very very quickly, so keep your eye on them – they're ready when they're just crispy. Enjoy as a yummy snack and know that you're doing your body good while still eating chips!

Sesame Lime Crunch Slaw

from Hailey

Dressing:
1/3 cup olive oil
4 Tbsp fresh ginger, finely chopped
2 Tbsp fresh garlic, finely chopped
3 Tbsp brown sugar
5 Tbsp soy sauce
4 Tbsp mirin (you can substitute with any white wine)
1 Tbsp sesame oil
1/4 cup rice wine vinegar (rice wine is ideal, but you can use any other type)
1 Tbsp lime juice, freshly squeezed
1 tsp red chili flakes

Vegetables: (shape is important for texture - you want it all cut very thin and roughly the same size)
1/2 large red cabbage, julienned
2 medium-sized carrots, julienned
1/2 large red onion, julienned
2 yellow peppers, julienned
1 red pepper, julienned
1 bunch bok choy, julienne the white stalks, and then finely chop the green part
handful bean sprouts
handful snap peas, cut the tips off, then cut in half
3 green onions stalks, chopped into 1/4" pieces
1/2 cup peanuts
1/2 cup sesame seeds, toasted (lightly shake them in a pan on med heat until they start to brown)
big handful crunchy noodles (buy them or make your own by frying vermicelli noodles in oil)
1 cup cilantro, rough chopped
3 limes, quartered

In a small saucepan add olive oil, ginger and garlic, and lightly sauté until lightly brown. Add brown sugar, soy sauce, and mirin. Sauté for 5 minutes and remove from heat. Then add sesame oil, rice wine vinegar, lime juice, and chili flakes.

Mix vegetables, and 3/4 of the peanuts, sesame seeds, noodles and coriander in a bowl and toss with dressing just before serving.

To garnish, put the rest of the sesame seeds, peanuts, noodles and coriander on top. Squeeze some fresh lime on, and place the quartered wedges on top for people to take as you serve the slaw.

Home Style Hummus & Pita Chips
from Martenia

Hummus:
1 can chickpeas
3 Tbsp tahini
½ lemon, juiced
2 garlic cloves
salt & pepper to taste

Put all the ingredients into a blender at a rate to ensure that they blend well. Purée until the desired smoothness is reached and enjoy!

Variation: Add a few dashes of cayenne pepper for a spicy kick, or 2 Tbsp of olive oil for a richer flavour!

Pita Chips:
4 large size pita breads ← *We like the thin pitas.*
3 Tbsp olive oil
pinch of thyme
pinch of cayenne pepper
1 Tbsp parsley
1 garlic clove, minced
1 Tbsp onion power
salt & pepper to taste

Preheat oven to 375°F

Cut pita bread into sections (about 8 wedges per pita). In a bowl, add garlic and spices to olive oil. Stir well. Brush or spoon olive oil with spices onto the pita pieces. Bake for about 7-12 minutes or until crisp. Watch they don't burn!

One time we took a road trip from Halifax to Toronto and this Hummus and these pita chips were our car snack. We took turns feeding each other while we drove.

Morro's Mean Lean Muffins
from Morro

1 cup unsweetened almond milk
1½ cups quick oats
½ cup brown sugar, packed
½ cup multigrain flour
½ tsp salt
½ tsp baking soda
1 tsp baking powder

2 Tbsp honey or agave
½ cup unsweetened applesauce
2 egg whites
1 Tbsp vegetable oil
1 tsp vanilla extract
1 cup blueberries
½ cup cranberries

Preheat oven 350°F

Pour the almond milk into the oats and, stir 'em up and give 'em a time out.

Grease muffin pans or line with parchment paper or your choice of pretty muffin papers. Mix up the sugar, flour, salt, baking soda and baking powder in a bowl. In another bowl, combine the honey, applesauce, egg whites, oil and vanilla extract. Then mix the oats n' almond milk mixture into the wet stuff.

Using your thumb or a spoon, make a well in the dry ingredients bowl and pour in the wet mixture. Stir them together but not too much – it's okay if there is still some powder showing. Fold in berries and divide the whole mix into the muffin cups. Bake for about 20 minutes, or until they start to brown on top and you pass the toothpick test.

I Can't Believe They're Not Cookies
from Morro

2 ripe bananas, mashed
1 cup quick oats
¼ cup semi-sweet chocolate chips

Preheat oven to 375°F

Combine ingredients. Spoon onto a nonstick cookie sheet and bake for 15 minutes or until firm. To spice things up, you can add a dash of cinnamon, vanilla, or substitute the chocolate chips for nuts, dried fruit, or any of your favorite toppings.

'What? I'm Eating My Veggies!' Zucchini Loaf
from Morro and Jasp

3 eggs
1 cup vegetable oil
1½ cups sugar
2 cups zucchini, finely grated and well drained
2 tsp vanilla extract
2 cups flour

1 tsp baking powder
¾ tsp baking soda
3 tsp cinnamon
1 tsp salt
1 cup raisins
1 cup walnuts

Preheat oven to 370°F

In a bowl, beat up the eggs (but don't hurt them) and then stir in oil, sugar, zucchini and vanilla. In another bowl, mix together the flour, baking powder, baking soda, cinnamon and salt. Then pour the dry ingredients into the wet ingredients and make sure they get along. Stir in the raisins and walnuts. Smell the batter. Yum...

Grease and flour a loaf pan and pour the yummy batter in. Bake it for 1 hour. Let it cool before removing it from the loaf pan – wait at least 10 minutes or the zucchini will be disappointed in your lack of patience.

BRAVE

When you feel like the world's greatest SuperHERO who can climb the highest mountain, swim the widest sea, cook the hardest recipe. You are the mighty albatross, the fierce lion, the rarest of unicorns.

BRAVO.

I'm Gonna Make You a Meatball You Can't Refuse

What's Your Hurry Lamb Curry Stew

Bring-It-On Bulgogi

Can You Handle the Heat, Jerk? Seasoning

Spinach. Cheese. Pie. Bam.

Captain Cabbage Rolls

Rad Pad Thai

Zen Zucchini and Mushroom Risotto

World's Best Lobster

The Fruit Bread of Destiny

Mighty Mabel's Rum Cake

Bewitching Brittle Banana Torte

Beet Generation Cake

Call me Super-morro.
Ready to take on
any reci-pie

morro get off of
the counter!

I'm Gonne Make You a Meatball You Can't Refuse
from Sue

Meatballs:
3 slices stale bread or 1½ cups breadcrumbs
milk, for soaking
2 eggs, beaten
1 Tbsp Worcestershire sauce
dash of Tabasco sauce
1 tsp salt
1 tsp dry mustard
1 garlic clove, minced
½ small onion, grated or finely chopped
fresh ground pepper to taste
1 lb lean ground beef or mixed ground beef and pork
1 cup fresh parmesan, grated

Sauce:
4¼ cups tomato purée or tomato sauce
1 cup water
2 bay leaves
1 garlic clove, minced
1 small onion, grated or finely chopped
1 tsp salt
pinch of cinnamon

If you want to make bigger balls cover them and cook 'em a bit longer

Soak the stale bread in milk and squeeze out the excess liquid. Add the eggs, Worcestershire, Tabasco, salt, mustard, minced garlic, onion and pepper. Add meat and parmesan and mix well. Let sit while preparing the sauce.

In a large pot bring to a boil the tomato purée, water, bay leaves, garlic and onion.

Make 1" meatballs out of the meat mixture and carefully drop each one into the tomato sauce until all the mixture is used up. Add a pinch of cinnamon and salt to taste and let simmer for about 30 minutes.

Serve with rice or pasta.

What's Your Hurry Lamb Curry Stew

from Chef Alan

Makes the whole house smell amazing!

3 lbs boneless lamb shoulder, cut into 2" cubes
3 Tbsp butter
1½ Tbsp vegetable oil
3 medium onions, diced
9 garlic cloves, chopped
3 Tbsp ginger, chopped
1 Tbsp cumin seeds
1½ tsp cinnamon
3 Tbsp paprika
1½ tsp crushed chilies
1 Tbsp thyme, fresh
1 Tbsp rosemary, fresh
3 bay leaves
2 Tbsp curry powder
3 cups canned tomatoes, chopped with juice
5 cups water
3 medium carrots, peeled and cut into 1" pieces
1 rutabaga, peeled and cut into 1" pieces
2 red peppers, chopped into 1" pieces
2 green peppers, chopped into 1" pieces
1 Tbsp olive oil
½ cup dried prunes or apricots, halved
2 cups couscous
salt & pepper to taste

Morro's veggie option: Use a can of drained chickpeas instead of lamb. But add them in with the carrots and rutabaga instead of at the start. Isn't rutabaga a fun word?!

Preheat oven to 350°F

Season lamb with salt and pepper and brown well in butter and vegetable oil in a large casserole or Dutch oven. Remove meat and in the remaining fat, cook onions until partly browned. Add garlic and ginger and cook 1 minute. Add spices and herbs and cook 1 minute more. Add tomatoes, water and browned lamb. Bring to a boil. Cover and cook in the oven for 1 hour.

Add carrots and rutabaga, and continue to cook for 45 minutes.

Sauté peppers separately in olive oil and add to stew along with dried fruit. Continue cooking for another 15 minutes.

Test lamb to make sure it's tender. Continue cooking if necessary. Serve over couscous, prepared according to package directions.

guess what?
Bulgogi means 'fire meat' in Korean.
It is usually made from thin slices of sirloin or prime cuts of beef.
Morro makes it with mushrooms instead of meat.

Bring-It-On Bulgogi
from Lauren

1/2 cup soy sauce
1/3 cup olive oil
3 garlic cloves, sliced
1 onion, sliced into strips
2 lbs beef, thinly sliced
1/3 cup sugar
salt & pepper to taste

In a large dish, combine soy sauce, olive oil, garlic and onions. Place beef slices in the dish, cover, and let marinate over night.

When you're ready to cook it, place the beef in a large pan and cook over medium heat until it is lightly browned. Then add the marinade and enough water so that it covers the top of the meat. Mix in sugar and heat it up until the liquid boils, then remove immediately. Add salt & pepper to taste.

Can You Handle the Heat Jerk Seasoning
from Martenia

You can make a fresh rub or a dry rub – the choice is yours!

Fresh rub:
2/3 cup Spanish onions, finely chopped
2 Tbsp lime juice
1 Tbsp salt
1 tsp red pepper, crushed
1 habanero pepper, finely diced
1/2 tsp allspice, ground
1/4 tsp black pepper
1/4 tsp curry powder
1/8 tsp thyme
1/8 tsp cayenne pepper
1/8 tsp ginger, ground fresh
2 garlic cloves, minced

Mix everything together. Spicy!

Dry rub:
2 tsp onion powder
2 Tbsp garlic powder
1 Tbsp chili flakes
2 tsp cayenne pepper
1 Tbsp salt
1/2 tsp allspice
1/4 tsp black pepper
1/4 tsp curry powder
1/8 tsp thyme
1/8 tsp ground ginger
2 Tbsp lime

Mix spices together and sprinkle on desired food item. Then squeeze lime juice on top.

Morro likes this on veggies. Jasp likes it on chicken. You decide!

Spinach. Cheese. Pie. Bam.
from Rick

Crust:
1 ¾ cups flour
1 tsp salt
1 tsp baking powder
⅓ cup olive oil
⅓ cup milk
1 egg

Filling:
1 Tbsp olive oil
1 onion, chopped
1 bunch green onions, chopped
10 oz package frozen spinach, drained
1 ½ cups feta cheese, crumbled
½ cup mozzarella, grated
2 eggs
½ cup mint, chopped
½ cup dill, chopped
½ cup parsley, chopped
1 ½ tsp salt
1 ½ tsp pepper
¼ tsp ground cloves

Preheat oven to 375°F

To make the crust, whisk together flour, salt and baking powder in a large bowl. In separate bowl, whisk oil, milk and egg and together. Pour the wet mix into the dry mix and stir until the dough is smooth. On a floured surface, knead the dough for 2 minutes or until it is smooth. Press it into a flat circle and wrap it in plastic. Refrigerate for 20 minutes.

To make the filling, heat olive oil over medium heat. Cook onions for about 2 minutes, or until softened, and then transfer into a large bowl. Add in the spinach, cheeses, eggs, mint, dill, parsley, salt, pepper and cloves and mix well.

On a floured surface, roll out the dough to make a large circle and place it in a 9" pie plate, letting the dough hang over the edges. Pour the filling in the centre and fold pastry over the filling, leaving an opening in the centre.

Bake it for about 45 minutes, or until the pastry is golden. Let stand for 10 minutes before serving.

If you want to make a larger dish for company, double the recipe and bake it in a 9x13" casserole dish.

Captain Cabbage Rolls
from Ramona

1 head of cabbage

Filling:
1 lb ground beef, uncooked
1 lb ground pork, uncooked
1 cup long grain rice, uncooked
1 large onion, diced
2 eggs
1 cup breadcrumbs

Sauce:
1 large can tomato sauce
1 large can diced tomatoes
¼ cup vinegar
¼ cup parsley
salt & pepper to taste

Preheat oven to 350°F

To prep the cabbage, cut out the core from the bottom and put it into a big pot of simmering water. As the individual leaves come away from the head, pull them out with tongs so they can cool. This softens them so they are prepped for rolling.

In a large mixing bowl, combine all the filling ingredients together. Roll the filling mixture in the cooled cabbage leaves. To make the sauce, heat all the ingredients in a pot and simmer for about 10 minutes. In a deep casserole dish (or 2, depending on the size), put a small layer of sauce over the bottom. Arrange the cabbage rolls in the dish with lots of sauce on top - be generous! Bake in the oven for 1½-2 hours, or until the cabbage is tender.

Morro's Veggie Option: Replace the beef and pork with this mixture!

¾ cup quinoa, uncooked
2 cups vegetable stock
2 cups mushrooms, coarsely chopped
2 garlic cloves, minced

1 Tbsp Worcestershire sauce
4 glugs olive oil
salt & pepper to taste

Cook the quinoa in the vegetable stock for 12-15 minutes, adding the mushrooms for the last 5 minutes. Add the other ingredients and then mix this with the rice, onions, eggs and breadcrumbs from the filling mixture listed above. Then carry on with the above recipe!

Rad Pad Thai
from Martenia

1 package tofu (firm works best), cubed
¼ cup olive oil
1 onion, slivered
1 pepper, red or green, chopped
3 eggs
1 package thin rice noodles or Pad Thai noodles
3-4 Tbsp tamarind paste
2 Tbsp fish sauce
2 tsp palm sugar (or brown sugar)
1-2 cups bean sprouts
4 green onions, chopped
peanuts, crushed to garnish
lime, cut into wedges to garnish

For this recipe you can use or omit tofu, chicken, shrimp or use all three!

In a large skillet pan, fry cubed tofu until golden and crispy. Add in onion and peppers. In a separate pan, scramble the eggs and then add to skillet. In a large pot, add noodles and 1 cup of water. Cover to steam. Once noodles are cooked, add tamarind paste, fish sauce and palm sugar. Stir until everything is well mixed. Add bean sprouts and green onions. Fry for 3-5 minutes, then cover and remove from heat. Add in everything from the skillet. Stir together and serve. Top with crushed peanuts and lime wedges.

Zen Zucchini and Mushroom Risotto
from Thom

2-3 zucchinis, diced
2-3 handfuls of mushrooms, diced (any kind you like best)
2-4 garlic cloves, diced
1/4 cup olive oil
8-10 cups stock, vegetable or chicken
2 cups Arborio rice
4-8 Tbsp parmesan, grated
salt & pepper to taste

In a large pot or stir fry pan, sauté the zucchini, mushroom and garlic in the olive oil over medium heat until tender. Add salt & pepper if you like, though I would recommend salt at least. In a separate pot, have the stock boiled and hot and ready.

Add Arborio rice to sautéed vegetables. Stir for 1-2 minutes, or until you can hear or smell the rice browning. Then add stock until all the rice is covered. From here on out, constantly and slowly, stir the rice.

When you can see the bottom of the pan, or can hear a sucking sound when you pass a spoon through the bottom of the pan, add more stock. Repeat 15-30 minutes, or until the rice is the consistency you like. Then stir in parmesan. Let it sit uncovered for at least 5 minutes before enjoying.

World's Best Lobster

from Morro and Jasp

Don't forget to thank the universe for the lobster and the fish. ♡

1 car (or train, or plane, or bike)
1 fishing license (lobster-specific)
1 fishing boat (bought or rented)
1 lobster trap
1 buoy

1 small fish, dead
1 lobster gauge
1 pair heavy-duty gloves
1 mess bag
1 ocean

To begin, travel to the east or west coast of wherever you are. If you don't have a coast near you, this part might take longer. (Before traveling, make sure you acquire the proper license to fish lobster. Certain governments are quite strict about this sort of thing and we don't want you to get in trouble.) Also, make sure to note how many lobsters you are allowed to catch at one time.

When you arrive on the coast, find the nearest fishing village, bait and tackle shop or marina. Hire a boat, or put your own into the water. (Note: make sure it's tied up to something on shore or it will float away.) Place traps, gloves, gauge and dead fish into your boat and set sail on the ocean.

It's important to know when to fish for lobsters – not only when they are in season but what time of the day is best to find them out and about. Lobsters generally hunt at night. In order to prep your lobster's 'new home' (okay, it's a trap), put the fish in the first compartment – most traps have two of these. Make sure your trap has an escape hole so that smaller lobsters that are too young to eat can get out. Some traps also have biodegradable panel that will dissolve after a while so that if the trap gets lost, the lobster won't die.

Make sure to write your name and license number on your traps before you put them in the water. Attach the buoy to the trap and lower away! Then wait. And wait. And wait. And wait some more. (It may be best to use a few traps, now that we're thinking about it.)

Upon checking the traps later in the day, if you discover you have located a lobster, make sure you use the gloves you brought – those guys can be pinchy. Measure your catch with the gauge to make sure it's regulation size. If it's not, throw him back. If he is, congrats! Place your lobster in mesh bag and head back to shore. Find a pot...and a stove (maybe a kind stranger will let you use theirs?) and steam your lobster in a large pot until ruby red. Then crack open and serve with clarified butter.

Alternatively, if you're on a coast already, there is probably a restaurant or something that serves lobsters. You could probably buy one there. Less fun, but far less work. It's up to you.

The Fruit Bread of Destiny
from Christina

- 1 tsp sugar
- 1 cup warm water (105-115°F)
- 4½ tsp active dry yeast (2 packages)
- ½ cup sugar
- ½ cup butter, melted
- 2 tsp salt
- 4 Tbsp vanilla extract
- ¼ cup lemon rind
- ¼ cup orange rind
- 6½ cups flour, divided
- 8 eggs
- 1 cup dried apricots, diced
- ½ cup dried cranberries
- ½ cup candied green cherries
- ½ cup candied red cherries

Add 1 tsp of sugar to warm water, then sprinkle yeast in water and let rise for 10 minutes. Once yeast has risen, stir down mixture and add ½ cup sugar, butter, salt, vanilla, lemon rind, orange rind and 2 cups of flour. Beat together with a mixer. Once combined, add eggs and gradually add remaining flour until it forms a ball. Place dough in a greased bowl, cover and set in a warm location. Let the dough rise until it doubles in size, about 2 hours.

Punch down dough and knead in diced apricots, cherries and cranberries. Shape dough in 2 loaves and place in 2 greased round cake pans. Cover and let rise until the dough doubles in size again.

Preheat oven to 350°F

Once the dough has risen, bake bread for 45-50 minutes or until it is golden in colour.

Mighty Mabel's Rum Cake
from Great Aunt Mabel

Cake:
- 3/4 cup butter
- 1 1/2 cups brown sugar
- 2 1/2 cups dates, chopped
- 1 cup walnut pieces
- 1 tsp baking soda
- 1 cup boiling water
- 2 eggs, beaten
- 1 1/2 cups flour
- 2-3 oz rum

Icing:
- 1 cup butter
- 2 1/2 cups icing sugar

Preheat oven to 350°F

To make the cake batter, cream 3/4 cup butter and add sugar, and then mix in dates and nuts. Add the baking soda to the boiling water and add the water with the dissolved baking soda to the butter mixture. Add the beaten eggs, flour and rum to the other ingredients and mix well. Pour the mixture into a greased angel food cake pan or bundt pan. Bake for 1 hour.

Now for the icing! Cream the butter and add in the icing sugar and keep creaming it until it looks and tastes like icing.

Turn out the cake from the pan & let cool. Spread the icing over top.

Bewitching Brittle Banana Torte
from Laurie

One of Jasp's favourites

Make sure to prepare this delectable torte at least a day before you want to serve it!

Dough:
1 cup butter
3 cups flour
1 cup sugar
1 tsp baking powder
1 egg

Peanut Brittle:
1 cup sugar
1 tsp butter
1/2 cup corn syrup
1 tsp vanilla extract
1 cup roasted & salted peanuts
1 tsp baking soda

Filling:
2 large packages cook & serve butterscotch pudding (not instant)
4 3/4 cups whole milk
5 large bananas
1 cup lemon juice
4 1/4 cups whipping cream
9 Tbsp icing sugar

To make the Dough:

Preheat the oven to 350°F

On 5 pieces of wax paper, trace a 9″ circle with your finger, and then cut each one out a finger's width bigger than the traced circle.

Cream the butter and sugar. Beat in the egg and add flour and baking powder and mix well. Refrigerate the dough for a few minutes so that it is easier to handle. Once chilled, divide the dough into 5 pieces (each approximately 6 1/2 oz) and pat each piece into a disc so that it fills the 9″ circle of wax paper.

Turn a 9″ cake pan upside down and place one of the wax bottomed discs on the outside bottom of the pan. Bake each layer for 10-15 minutes until golden, but watch the layers carefully after 10 minutes. Repeat this for each of the 5 layers. Once baked, remove the layers from oven and immediately slide onto a cooling rack. Place a second cooling rack on top of the layer so that you can flip the layer over and remove the wax paper. Let the torte layers cool for 10 minutes before moving them (they are very delicate).

To make the Peanut Brittle:

This peanut brittle is made in the microwave so that it is light and airy, which is best for this torte. In an 8 1/2 x 11″ microwave safe casserole dish, stir together sugar and syrup. Microwave at high for 4 minutes. Then stir in peanuts and microwave again at high for 4 minutes. Add butter and vanilla to mixture and blend well, then microwave at high for 1 1/2 minutes. Quickly add baking soda and gently stir until light and foamy. Pour mixture onto a lightly greased cookie sheet. Let cool for 30-60 minutes. Break peanut brittle into small pieces using a rolling pin. Keep cool or frozen until needed.

To make the Filling:

Combine pudding powder and milk. Whisk until well blended. Cook pudding in microwave or on the stove at a high temperature until the mixture boils. Stir every 2 minutes to prevent lumps. Once mixture boils, remove from microwave or stove. Cool for 10 minutes, then stir and cover with plastic. Allow it to cool completely before using.

Slice bananas and place them in lemon juice. (The lemon flavour adds to the taste of the torte and prevents the bananas from turning black.) Remove from juice and strain well.

Place a mixing bowl and beaters in the freezer for at least 10 minutes. Pour whipping cream and icing sugar in chilled bowl and whip. Beat until cream is very thick and stiff. Refrigerate uncovered until needed.

To assemble the Torte:

Spread some whipped cream on the bottom of one torte layer and place on a large glass plate. Spread 1 cup of pudding on top of the layer. On top of the pudding, place enough banana slices to totally cover the pudding. Place the next torte layer on top of the bananas and cover with 1 cup of pudding and then a layer of banana slices. Repeat these layers two more times. Then, place the last torte layer on top and spread on a layer of whipped cream. Then cover sides of the torte with whipped cream, making sure the entire torte is covered.

Refrigerate the torte and remaining whipped cream overnight, making sure they are both uncovered (very important!). The next morning, add additional whipped cream to the top and sides of torte. Then cover sides of torte with small crumbs of peanut brittle and use larger pieces for the top.

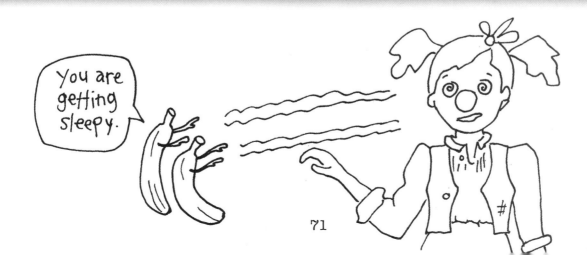

Dear fruit flies,

Really?

Don't get me wrong, each creature has the right to exist, but come on. You're kinda killing my summer buzz, man.

And sure, you've got some impressive things on your resume. You can beat your wings up to 220 times per second, and you have 760 eye 'units' (whatever that means), and maybe you are one of the most studied living creatures ever, but man, are you a party crasher!

So there I was, just having a nice evening and in you come, no RSVP or nothing. And as I was enjoying my sliced melon, you thought "that looks good, maybe I'll just fly on over and have myself a taste", and landed right on top of the piece I was in the middle of eating.

But that's not all, you managed to tell your friends about my generosity, 'cause the next day, there were 3 more of you INSIDE my kitchen. Now, I'm as welcoming as the next clown, but you didn't even knock!

And now? And now, here we are. I came downstairs this morning and what did I find? 12, count them 12 of you, just hanging around my before-bed chocolate milk goblet (that Morro was supposed to wash but didn't). You all looked like you were having quite the party.

Enough is enough. I'm done here. You've gone too far this time. When next we meet, it's war. War I tell ya!

Consider yourself warned.

~Jasp.

← The fruit fly

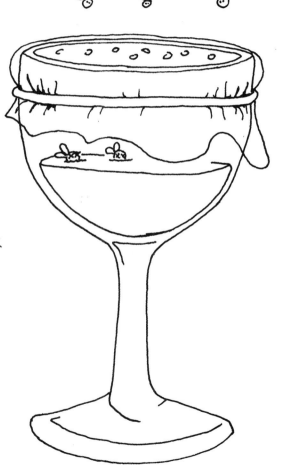

How to make a Trap

1. Put some wine, ripe fruit and liquid or apple cider vinegar into a glass.

2. Tightly fit cellophane wrap or a plastic bag around the top of the glass and secure it with an elastic band.

3. Poke holes in the plastic with a fork or a toothpick (small holes just big enough to let the flies in).

4. Wait while the juices attract the flies and they are lured to your trap.

muah ha ha!

Beet Generation Cake
from Morro and Jasp

Cake:
3 oz unsweetened chocolate, chopped
2 cups sugar
4 eggs
1½ cups vegetable oil
1½ tsp vanilla extract
2 cups flour
2¼ tsp baking soda
¼ tsp salt
3 x 12 oz cans beets, drained and puréed
(NOT PICKLED BEETS!!!)

Icing:
1-2 cups heavy cream
12 oz cream cheese, room temperature
1½ cups mascarpone cheese
½ tsp vanilla extract
1½ cups icing sugar, sifted

Preheat oven to 350°F

Melt chocolate in a double boiler. In another bowl, mix sugar, eggs, oil and vanilla together. In another large bowl, sift together flour, baking soda and salt. Add the dry ingredients to the wet ingredients and mix well. Slowly add the melted chocolate into the mixture and blend. Add the puréed beets (but don't spill them on yourself – they totally stain) and mix until everything is well blended. Pour cake batter into three greased and floured cake pans and bake for 20-25 minutes. Let the cakes cool and then turn them out onto a cooling rack.

To make the icing, pour the cream into a small bowl and whip well (the more whipped cream, the fluffier the icing will be). Refrigerate the whipped cream. Mix the cream cheese until smooth. Add in the mascarpone and mix. Stir in the vanilla and icing sugar. Fold in the whipped cream and refrigerate until it's time to put the cake together. Then layer the icing between the three cakes, so you have a three layered cake for triple the fun. Ice the top and sides of the cake and sprinkle it with something pretty like cocoa powder, chocolate shavings, or wherever the groove takes you, man...

The Cycle of Life
By MORRO

First you were a tiny seed (yes it's true, so small indeed)
And when you slowly began to sprout (you poked your very first leaves out)
You reached towards the warm sunlight (and felt all strong and proud and bright)
And up and up and up you grew (and drank in the fresh, sweet morning dew)

Soon you rose up big and strong (it didn't really take that long)
And when you felt the time was right (it really was quite a pretty sight)
You let loose seeds of your very own (so that you'd never be alone)
And so the cycle began anew (and now there's many instead of just a few)

From seed to tree, from tree to seed (that's how it works, it is indeed)
You've shown me how things start and end (and also become an important friend)
Soooooo
Now I see you every day (and say hello when I pass your way)
I thank you for the wisdom you gave (your lessons I will always save)
I love you trees, I really do (and thank you lots for loving me too)

Romantical

When you want to impress the pants off someone. Literally.

Easy Peasy Rosy Posey Sangria

Dandy Brandy Red Sangria

White Fuzzy Peach Sangria

Show Me Your (Red Thai Curry) Mussels

Cheese Fawn-Over-You-Due

Cupid's Caprese Salad

Caes(ar) the Night Salad with Take My Breath Away Croutons

Come and Getta Bruschetta

Moonlight Sonata Ricotta Gnocchi

Super Sexy Seductive Soufflé

Balls, Coconut Balls

Juliet's Love Letters

Sassy Flourless Chocolate Cake

Classy Chocolate Ganache

Easy Peasy Rosy Posey Sangria
from Jasp

1 bottle rosé wine
1 can frozen pink lemonade
2 cups frozen berries
2 cups ginger ale or ginger beer
1 cup soda water

Throw it all in a punch bowl and mix it up.
Yummy in my tummy read-to-go sangria.

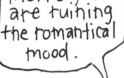

"morro you are ruining the romantical mood."

Dandy Brandy Red Sangria
from Laura

1-2 cups brandy
2-3 oranges, cut into rounds
2-3 lemons, cut into rounds
2-3 limes, cut into rounds
2-3 apples, cored and cut into chunks
1-2 cups orange juice
2 bottles red wine
2 cups sparkling water

Place cut fruit in a large bowl or container and pour in enough brandy to cover all of the fruit. Cover and let sit overnight to allow the fruit to absorb the liquor.

The next day, mix the fruit and brandy with orange juice, wine and sparkling water. Serve to your lucky lucky friends.

White Fuzzy Peach Sangria
from Morro

1 bottle white wine
¾ cup peach schnapps
¼ cup vodka
3 fresh peaches, sliced and pitted
1 orange or tangerine, sliced
1 large bottle soda water
any of your other favorite fruits

In a large punch bowl or pitcher, mix together all the ingredients. Add the soda water just before serving. Enjoy responsibly!

Show Me Your (Red Thai Curry) Mussels
from Stacy-Lee

3 lbs mussels, cleaned and debearded
¼ cup butter
6 plum tomatoes, chopped
1 medium sweet onion, chopped
4 garlic cloves, minced
1 Tbsp fresh ginger, chopped
2 x 14 oz cans unsweetened coconut milk
1-2 Tbsp Thai red curry paste
¼ cup fresh cilantro, chopped
1 tsp salt

Or coconut cream if you want to impress a special someone!

In a large pan or pot, melt the butter over medium heat. Add tomatoes, onion, garlic and ginger. Sauté until tender.

Add coconut milk, curry paste, cilantro, and salt. Simmer for an additional 5 minutes. Add mussels, then cover and cook for another 5 minutes or until the mussels are opened. Make sure to discard any mussels that are not opened! They are bad!

Plate and serve immediately. For maximum effect, enjoy with red wine and hot crusty bread for dipping.

Cheese Fawn-Over-You-Due

from Lynne

1 cup dry white wine
2 Tbsp flour
1/4 tsp salt
1/2 lb Swiss cheese
1/2 lb Gruyere cheese
pinch of nutmeg
1 loaf French bread, cut into cubes

In a saucepan on the stove, heat the wine and then slowly add the flour and salt and whisk to make a rue. Add the cheese in small amounts and melt slowly over medium heat. Do not let it boil. When all the cheese is melted, transfer the mixture to a fondue pot and add the nutmeg.

Serve with the bread cubes poked onto the fondue forks. When you dip your bread in the fondue, keep stirring the mixture in a figure 8 to keep it soft and melty.

Variation: You can use other cheeses like brie for a sweeter fondue!

Requirement: Have your guests pretend to fence with the fondue forks! Enjoy the mayhem and fun and don't burn your tongue on the hot cheese!

An Ode to Cheese ♡
By Jasp

Be you
Squeaky
or salty
or sharp
or soft
or silky
or spicy
or smoked
or shredded...

you complete me.

Cupid's Caprese Salad
from Morro and Jasp

1 cup balsamic vinegar
2 Tbsp brown sugar ← or honey instead
1 tsp soy sauce
4 tomatoes, sliced
6 bocconcini cheese balls, sliced
20 fresh basil leaves
1 Tbsp olive oil

In a medium sized pot, bring the balsamic vinegar and sugar to a boil. Reduce heat and let simmer for 15 minutes or until you notice it thickening. Don't let it fully caramelize. Otherwise it won't pour nicely and you'll be sad that you messed up. Add in soy sauce towards the end. Let cool for 5 minutes before serving.

On a plate, layer tomato then cheese then basil. Make sure you do it in that order or...well, we take no responsibility for what happens if you don't. Then drizzle the reduction and olive oil over top. The balsamic is strong, so start with a little and add more if you need!

Caes(ar) the Night Salad with Take My Breath Away Croutons
from Matt

You can use capers instead for a veggie option →

Caesar Salad Dressing:
- 1 Tbsp dijon mustard
- 3 garlic cloves, minced
- 1/4 cup fresh parmesan, grated
- 1 1/2 Tbsp anchovy paste or capers
- 1 1/2 Tbsp fresh lemon juice
- 1/2 tsp white wine vinegar
- 2 tsp Worcestershire sauce
- 1 egg yolk
- 3/4 cup canola or olive oil

Mix the dijon, garlic, parmesan, anchovy paste or capers, lemon juice, vinegar, Worcestershire sauce and egg yolk together. Then slowly add the oil to emulsify the dressing. You can either use a food processor or whisk in a glass bowl – it's up to you!

↳ Add it all to some romaine lettuce or kale for a fun twist.

Garlic Confit Oil:
- 1 cup garlic cloves, peeled and cleaned.
- olive oil

Put garlic in a pot and fill with enough oil to cover the garlic cloves by 1". Cook over medium-low heat (use a diffuser if necessary, bubbles should rise but not break the surface) stirring every 5 minutes for about 40 minutes. Remove from heat and let cool, then jar the oil.

Fancy Croutons:
- 1 bread loaf, fresh (country or sourdough)
- 4-6 Tbsp garlic confit oil
- 2 Tbsp butter
- salt & pepper to taste
- paprika (optional)

Tear the bread into pieces or cube it with a knife. (Stale bread can also be used but will have different consistency.) Add the bread pieces to a bowl with a few Tbsp of the oil and mix with salt & pepper to taste. In a large frying pan add confit oil until you've filled up about 1/8 of the pan. Heat the oil and add the butter. The oil should be hot but not smoking. Add the bread pieces in an even layer and fry until golden and crispy on all sides. Remove from oil and place on salad or enjoy as a garlicky snack!

Come and Getta Bruschetta
from Stacy-Lee

6 plum tomatoes, diced
1/3 medium-sized red onion, diced
2 garlic cloves, diced
7 fresh basil leaves, chopped

1 Tbsp olive oil
1 tsp balsamic vinegar
1 cup parmesan, grated
1 fresh and crispy baguette

Preheat oven to 375°F

Combine tomato, red onion, garlic, basil leaves, olive oil, and balsamic vinegar in a bowl and lightly toss.

Slice baguette and top with bruschetta mix. Sprinkle with freshly grated parmesan and bake for 10 minutes. Serve warm.

Variation: Use fresh parsley instead of basil, or add diced sundried tomatoes to your bruschetta.

Best to use real parmesan cheese, not the shakey kind.

Moonlight Sonata Ricotta Gnocchi

from Jessica

Pasta:
8 oz extra fine ricotta cheese, drained
2 eggs
½ cup parmesan
1 cup flour
2 shakes of salt

Other Stuff:
2 cups flat parsley
2 cups fresh basil
4 garlic cloves
½ cup pine nuts, divided
½ cup extra virgin olive oil
salt to taste
asiago, grated
fresh ground pepper

Mix together ingredients for dough: ricotta, eggs, parmesan, flour and salt. You may need to add more flour – you should be able to roll it without it sticking to your hand. Divide the dough into 3 or 4 pieces, and roll into ½" thick ropes on a floured surface. Cut each rope up into 1" pieces of gnocchi.

Mix in a blender, food processor, or finely chop parsley, basil, garlic and ¼ cup pine nuts. Mix in olive oil and salt to taste. Presto! You just made pesto!!! Heat pesto mixture in a large skillet at medium heat.

Boil gnocchi in large pot of salted water so they don't stick together. Don't add oil to the water. The gnocchi is ready as soon as it floats to the top of the water. Don't overcook. With a slotted spoon add cooked gnocchi to hot pesto in skillet. Add remaining pine nuts, asiago and fresh pepper to garnish.

Guess what! "Gnocchi" might get its name from the Italian "nocchio" meaning "a knot in wood" or from "nocca" meaning "knuckle".
In the Roman Era this pasta spread all over Europe and Asia. That's why there are so many kinds of gnocchi - some with potatoes or even with breadcrumbs like in Venice ♡

Pesto is usually made with cheese and nuts too but those come later here.

Super Sexy Seductive Soufflé
from Jasp

The late great Virginia Woolf once said, "One cannot think well, love well, sleep well, if one has not dined well." And I, personally, agree. I believe it was her who also said "The way to a man's heart is through his stomach." And so, I have carefully crafted a recipe, designed to make any man fall in love on first bite!

1 cup cereal (works best with the sugary kind he ate when he was young)
1/3 cup coffee from his favourite coffee shop
4 marshmallows, melted (make sure to take them out of the bag first)
1 Tbsp peanut butter (but make sure he's not allergic)
1 slice of white bread, crusts removed (it's gotta be white bread - trust me)
1 pickle, plus juice
1 Tbsp mayonnaise (the greatest of the condiments)
1 can oysters (they will make you feel... nice)
3 Vienna sausages (because boys like sausage parties)
dash of cayenne pepper
pinch of cocoa powder
drop of red food colouring (to make things pretty and pink)
a shake of medicinal cannabis (medicinal kind only, people)
salt & pepper to taste

To garnish:
1/3 cup whipped cream (I like the squirty kind)
1 maraschino cherry (boys also like cherries)
1 sparkler (for flair)

> But don't forget to add the stuff that boys Actually like:
> - A handful of cheeesies (the puffed kind, not the crunchy ones - they are weird)
> - 1/2 Can of beer
> - 2 Strips of bacon
> from MoRRo
> xo

To begin, get yourself a nice, big mixing bowl – the nicer looking the better. Form is content, right? Right.

Starting at the beginning of the list, add one ingredient at a time. The order is REALLY important. These are all things boys like and boys are picky and sometimes difficult to understand so you have to be extra careful to not mess it up or make them run away when you try to feed...or serve it to them, rather.

When all the ingredients have been properly assembled, and a fine balance of taste and texture has been achieved, it's time to plate! I personally prefer a glass sundae-style dish as it allows you to see all the exciting things inside.

Once it is plated, top with whipped cream and a cherry. Then all you have to do is light the sparkler and get ready to impress your future man! (If you already have a man, then why are you even reading this? You don't need this. Hasn't life been good enough to you already?)

Note from Jasp: never let Morro near your special recipes or this is what happens
Note from Morro: I'm Just helping!
Note from Jasp again: No you aren't!
WAIT!
Get into the bucket my pretty. muah ha ha!
cereal
CHEESIES
flour
SALT
Morro & Jasp's KITCHEN

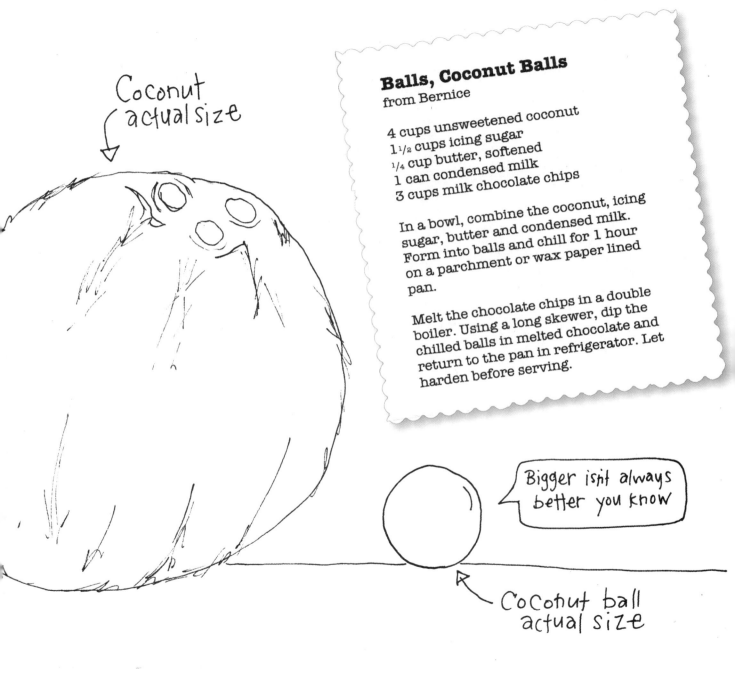

Juliet's Love Letters
from Sheena and Sean

2 cups raspberries
1 cup sugar, divided
1/4 cup butter
1 cup white baking chocolate, divided
2 eggs
1 cup flour
1/2 tsp salt

♡ for hopelessly sweet romantics ... or star-crossed lovers ... either way works ♡

Preheat oven to 325°F

Put the raspberries in a pot on the stove and add 1/2 cup sugar and simmer on medium heat for around 15 minutes, or until the mixture thickens to a jam consistency. Stir frequently so it does not burn.

In a double boiler, melt butter and 1/2 cup white chocolate and stir until smooth.

In a large bowl, beat eggs until foamy and slowly mix in the remaining sugar. Keep beating mixture while slowly adding in melted chocolate. Then stir in flour and salt. Chop the remaining chocolate, and mix into bowl.

Layer half of the mix into a greased and floured 8" square pan. Layer the jam over the mix already in the pan. Use the remaining half of the mix to roughly cover the jam layer, then use a knife to marble the mix and jam to make it pretty.

Bake for 30-35 minutes. Do the toothpick test! After it has cooled, cut it into squares.

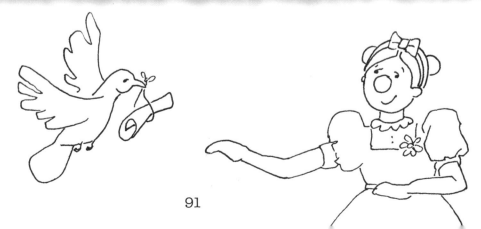

Sassy Flourless Chocolate Cake
from Morro

7 oz dark chocolate
2/3 cup butter
5 eggs, separated
2/3 cup golden caster sugar

3 Tbsp strong coffee, instant or brewed
1 cup almond flour
2 Tbsp cocoa powder, unsweetened
1 tsp baking powder

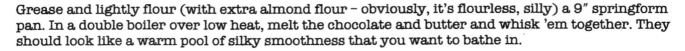

Preheat oven to 375°F

Grease and lightly flour (with extra almond flour – obviously, it's flourless, silly) a 9" springform pan. In a double boiler over low heat, melt the chocolate and butter and whisk 'em together. They should look like a warm pool of silky smoothness that you want to bathe in.

Beat the egg whites with a mixer until they're nice and stiff (when you can tip the bowl on its side and they don't go anywhere, you're good to go). Then pour half of the sugar in and beat it together.

Add the other half of the sugar to the egg yo-yo-yolks and beat 'em together until they're all creamy and thick. Add it to the melted chocolate, along with the coffee (don't get tired and drink it), and gently stir it all together. Delicately (this one is hard for me) fold the beaten egg whites into the mix, making sure that the air beaten into them doesn't get lost. (Remember how hard you worked to beat those eggs? Why would you throw it all away now?) Don't overmix it or you will have a sad, flat cake and nobody wants that. You still want little bits of powdery goodness showing.

Mix together the almond flour, cocoa powder and baking powder, then slowly add this dry stuff to the wet chocolaty mix. Mix it up, but don't beat it – delicate, remember? Pour the mixture into the springform and bake it for 45-50 minutes. Do the toothpick test but make sure you don't overcook it, 'cuz the cake should be moist and delectable. Leave the cake in the springform for 30-ish minutes to cool, then cool it on a wire rack...or a plate.

Before serving, dust it with cocoa powder or smother it in Classy Chocolate Ganache.

Classy Chocolate Ganache
from Morro

1 cup whipping cream or plain unsweetened soy milk
8 oz dark or semisweet chocolate, broken into small pieces

Place the unwhipped whipping cream and the chocolate in a double boiler. Keep stirring it until it's all melted together. As soon as it is smooth and velvety, immediately drizzle or smother it on the Sassy Cake.

Dear Mystery Lover,

Your eyes are more beautiful and deeper than the deepest ocean
Columbus would have given it all up if he sailed upon them.
Your skin is as soft as a kitten's ear
But I'm not allergic to it, so it's even better.
Your lips are two pink pillows
That I would love to nap on (but I'm too busy writing you a love poem)
Your hair is silky like a chemise I once had
Where did that go? It was such a beautiful colour...
But not as beautiful as your soul
Which beams with powerful, powerful rays of awesome
But that don't hurt or kill people like light sabers
Your heart is like no other I have ever seen
Although, I've never actually seen a real live heart
Because if I had it would mean I was a doctor or a killer
Which I most certainly am not
I am just a clown
Who is madly in love with all of the lovely things
About you.

♡ Jase

heartbroken

When you feel like whoever said it's better to have loved than lost is a big FAT liar... sob... sniffle...

Tough Day Truffle Mac & Cheese

Tougher Day Tomato Mac & Cheese

Cried My Eyes Out Chocolate Cake

Why'd Ya Cheat On Me Cheesecake

Heal My Heart With Cheese Potatoes

Pick-Me-Up Peanut Butter Cookie Dough

Tough Day Truffle Mac & Cheese
from Jasp

8 oz macaroni	1 cup cream
1/4 cup butter	1 cup sharp cheddar cheese (your favourite kind), grated
1/4 cup flour	1/2 cup gruyere or asiago (whichever you like better), grated
1/2 tsp salt	3/4 cup parmesan, grated and divided
pepper to taste	1-2 tsp truffle oil or shaved truffles
1 cup milk	1/2 cup breadcrumbs

Preheat oven to 400°F

Cook the macaroni noodles in boiling hot water – I'm assuming you've cooked noodles before. Don't overcook them, silly.

To make a roux, melt the butter in a very large saucepan, whisking in the flour with salt & pepper until it's all blended. Slowly add the milk and cream and keep on whisking. Is your wrist tired? Too bad, yummy sauce means serious whisking. Bring to a low boil and let it boil for 2 minutes. Make sure it doesn't burn to the pan, which means – you guessed it - more whisking! Then lower heat and cook for another 10 minutes, or until the roux is thickened, whisking the whole entire time. Slowly add in the cheddar, gruyere or asiago, and 1/2 cup parmesan a little bit at a time. Simmer the cheeses in the roux for another 5 minutes, or until the cheese melts. Don't forget to whisk.

Turn off the heat and add the macaroni into the cheesy sauce. With tender love, add your truffle. The more you put the more it will heal your aching soul. But start with a little, then mix everything together. Smell it. If it smells like it needs more truffle love, add more. Make sure the noodles and sauce are mixed well together then scoop it all into a buttered casserole dish. Mix the breadcrumbs with the remaining parmesan. Smother the top with this mixture and bake it for about 20 minutes or until the top is crispy and golden.

Tougher Day Tomato Mac & Cheese
from Kevin and Heidi

Morro's fave mac & cheezze

1 lb elbow macaroni, cooked al dente
28 oz can diced tomatoes
6 Tbsp unsalted butter
1/2 cup flour
1/2 tsp cayenne pepper
4 cups half and half cream
1 cup vegetable broth
4 cups mild cheddar cheese, shredded
2 cups sharp cheddar cheese, shredded
salt & pepper to taste

Topping:
1/3 cup breadcrumbs
1 tsp garlic powder
1/2 tsp cayenne pepper
1/4 cup parmesan, grated
2 glugs olive oil

Preheat oven to 400°F

In a large pot, pour diced tomatoes with juice over cooked macaroni and stir to coat. Cook over medium heat until most of the liquid is absorbed, or about 5 minutes, then set aside.

In a medium saucepan, melt butter over medium heat until foaming. Stir in flour and cayenne and cook for about 1 minute or until golden. Slowly whisk in the broth and half and half cream until smooth. Bring to a boil, reduce heat to medium and simmer, stirring occasionally until mixture is slightly thickened. Take off heat and whisk in both types of cheeses and salt & pepper to taste.

Pour cheese sauce over macaroni and scrape into a large baking dish. In a separate bowl, mix breadcrumbs, garlic powder, cayenne, grated parmesan and olive oil to make it all stick together. Then crumble this mixture over the macaroni. Bake for 15-20 minutes, or until browned.

Cried My Eyes Out Chocolate Cake

from Morro and Jasp

Cake:
4 oz semi-sweet baking chocolate
2½ cups flour, sifted
1½ cups sugar
1 tsp baking soda
½ tsp baking powder
½ tsp salt
⅔ cup butter, softened
1 cup buttermilk, divided
1 tsp vanilla extract
2 eggs

Icing:
1 cup evaporated milk
1 cup sugar
3 egg yolks, slightly beaten
½ cup butter
1 tsp vanilla extract
1½ cups flaked coconut
1 cup pecans, chopped

Preheat oven to 350°F

Melt chocolate in a double boiler then set it aside. Do NOT cry into the chocolate, or it won't be smooth (we know – it's hard).

In a bowl, sift flour with sugar, baking soda, baking powder and salt. In yet another bowl, stir butter until softened. You can beat it if you want – it might help you through your tough time. Add the butter into the flour mixture, along with ¾ cup of the buttermilk and the vanilla. Mix to dampen flour and then beat it for 2 minutes. Add melted chocolate, eggs and remainder of the buttermilk into the mix. Beat for another minute – come on, get it out of your system. Pour the batter into 3 greased and floured 8″ pans (round, square, or heart-shaped pans – if yours is still intact, that is). Bake for 30-35 minutes, and do the toothpick test. Cool in the pans for 15 minutes and then remove and cool on wire racks.

While the cake is baking, make the icing (trust us, the icing is important in the healing process). Mix up the evaporated milk, sugar, egg yolks, butter and vanilla in saucepan. Cook it up over medium heat until it gets thick and gooey (just like your feelings) for about 12 minutes. And stir it – don't forget about it and ignore (like how s/he did). Remove it from heat – don't burn it (like s/he did to you). Mix in coconut and pecans. Let the icing cool until it's spreadable. Beat it every now and then – that feels better already, doesn't it? Spread the icing on the cake layers and make them into a 3-tiered tower of heartbreak, hope, and happiness. Cover the entire cake in icing and then go at it with a fork – why bother with plates? Actually, why bother with a fork? Just get in there and get chocolatey. Make sure to eat it with at least one other person (your sister, for example).

The Best Medicine
By Morro & Jasp

Chocolate cake, we love you so.
When life's the worst we always know
That you'll be there no matter what.
From the tips of our tongue to depths of our gut.
You fill us up with the best kind of feeling.
From you we find the source for our healing.
Flourless, fudge, or devil's food
You know how to put us in the right kind of mood.
So next time our hearts are full of ache
We know we'll reach for a piece of cake.

Why'd Ya Cheat On Me Cheesecake
from Laurie

Crust:
2 cups graham crackers, crushed
4 Tbsp butter, melted

Filling:
24 oz cream cheese
1 cup sugar
4 eggs, separated
1 tsp vanilla extract

Topping:
2 cups sour cream
1 tsp vanilla extract
2 Tbsp sugar

Preheat oven to 350°F

Mix graham cracker crumbs and butter, and use to line the bottom and sides of a greased 9" springform pan. Mix cream cheese with sugar, egg yolks and vanilla until smooth. In a separate bowl, beat the egg whites until they are stiff and then gently fold them into the cheese mixture. Pour this mixture onto the crust. Bake for 40-50 minutes then remove from the oven. Increase the temperature to 475°F. Blend the topping ingredients and gently spoon over cake. Return cake to the oven and bake for 5 more minutes. The topping won't be set yet, but don't worry! Remove cheesecake from the oven and cool to room temperature. Refrigerate overnight. You can eat it plain or add any fruit topping you want!

Did you know that cheesecake heals your heart? It's true... Just ask us.

Heal My Heart With Cheese Potatoes
from Mark

6 large potatoes ← Yukon gold are great, but any potatoes will work.
1 cup sour cream
2 cups sharp cheddar cheese, shredded and divided
1 bunch green onions, chopped
4 oz cream cheese, grated
½ tsp salt
½ tsp pepper
paprika

Preheat oven to 350°F

Cook the potatoes in their skins in boiling water until fork tender. Let the potatoes cool slightly and peel the skins off. Grate the peeled potatoes into a large bowl. Stir in sour cream, 1½ cups of the grated cheddar, onions, cream cheese, salt and pepper. Transfer the potato mixture into a buttered casserole dish. Top with the remaining cheddar cheese and sprinkle with paprika. Bake, uncovered for about 30-40 minutes, or until heated through.

Dearest Diary,

Today was revolutionary. You know how I've been experimenting with creativity lately? Well today I reached the precipice of a point of no looking back from that sort of in-the-box style thinking people like "the man" encourage you to do and began my intellectual revolution.

Today I invented a recipe.

Okay, the morning did not start off in such a positive way. It was really terrible, actually. I had a bit of a cheese hangover after gorging last night in reaction to Jordan Collington not answering my phone call. Okay, phone calls. And then when he finally answered (I thought maybe his ringer was off) he told me I needed help. So I got help. Morro fed me cheese while I cried and then passed out on the couch.

When I woke up this morning, I felt like I needed to make myself feel better with something new. Something different and extraordinary. So I went into the kitchen and found the bag of chocolate chips. Then I opened the pantry and saw the crispy rice and the marshmallows. Then

From Jasp's Journal

I opened the fridge and saw the chocolate milk and the slightly overripe banana. Then I opened the cracker drawer and saw the graham crackers - And then it hit me. These things were all made to be together.

All the sweet things in life belong together. So I helped them fulfill their destiny. I put them all in a bowl, mixed them together, and heated them up in the microwave. Then I put them in the freezer to truly bond together And they did. They became this one amazing entity that I put my fork into and it was a little tough due to their frozen nature - but that's the point, isn't it? They bonded stronger, better and more delicious. The sensation filled my mouth with joy and liberation, and the realization that I am one of the great minds of my generation.

So now I go into the world, diary. I go to fulfill my destiny and find the sweet tasting souls who will partner with me to sprinkle wonder and delight into the universe through this delicious transformation. Move over Einstein, Edison and Betty Crocker. Jasp has taken the reigns.

Jasp ♡

Pick-Me-Up Peanut Butter Cookie Dough
from Lynn

1 cup sifted flour
1/4 tsp salt
2 tsp baking powder
3 Tbsp shortening or butter
3 heaping Tbsp peanut butter
1/2 cup brown sugar
1 egg, well beaten
1 tsp vanilla extract
3/4 cup mixed nuts, ground (optional)
1/4 cup white sugar (for coating the cookies)

Combine flour, salt and baking powder in a large bowl and set aside. In another bowl, cream shortening or butter, peanut butter and sugar until fluffy. Add egg and vanilla and cream together well. Add the peanut butter mixture to the dry ingredients and mix together, finally adding in the ground nuts as you do so.

Take a Tbsp of the dough and roll it into a ball in your hand. Dunk the dough ball in the white sugar until coated to your taste. Place these onto a greased baking sheet and flatten each ball with a fork.

Or just eat it right now. Do not overstuff yourself. It will feel good in the moment, but really really the opposite of good after you have a belly full of raw cookie dough. But it does stop the tears for a while, and if it doesn't, you will have gooier, saltier cookie dough and that's never a bad thing.

If you feel like you want to be civilized, you can bake them at 350°F for 9-15 minutes, depending on how chewy or crispy you want them.

And then eat the whole batch.

MORRO'S SORROW

There's a hole in my heart... Several actually. They hurt a lot.

I think they are growing and it makes it hard to breathe.

What's the point of giving your heart away if it only ever comes back broken and tattered, and torn and with growing cesspools of hole-ness?

Life is salty... just like my tears.

ANGRY!

When you feel like everyone else is wrong and the world sucks and you just want to break something!...%.#@&!

What are you looking AT?!

Homemade Wine
from Morro and Jasp

Ingredients:
1000 grapes

Note: If you want red wine, use red grapes. If you want white wine, use green grapes. Don't go looking for white grapes. They do not exist. Trust us.

You will need a giant tub that is structurally sound. Put the grapes in the tub. Take off your shoes AND your socks. Wash your feet.

Think about all the things that really suck in life and get in the tub and stomp. Stomp and stomp and stomp some more until you get all that rage out of your system. You can jump if you want, but that may lead to feelings of fun, so if you want to stay angry, you should probably keep stomping.

When all the grapes are sufficiently stomped, step out of the tub. Wash off your feet and dry them well.

Wait 3-5 years.

Wine.

I need a Snuggle

When you feel tired and stressed... and you've had a rough day... and you feel a cold coming on... and you're bloated and menstrual... and your socks are soaked because you have holes in your rubber boots and you stepped in a puddle... and all you need is for your food to give you a big, comforting hug.

Waaaahhh

Spicy Coconut Lentil Soup

The Pretty Soup

What's the Dilly Pickle Soup

Oodles of Noodles and Beans Soup

Belly Full o' Black Bean Soup

Drunken Mushroom Stew

Doughboy Dumplings

Enchilada Lasagna Casserole Layered Goodness

Bengali-Style Chicken Curry

Chana My-Sala

Southern Cheese Grits

Cod au Gratin

Better Than Your Mom's Lasagna

Spicy Coconut Lentil Soup
from Elise

3 tsp sunflower or canola oil
1 vidalia or spanish onion, diced
6 garlic cloves, minced
2 tsp fresh ginger, grated
1 tsp curry powder
1 tsp ground cumin
1 tsp ground coriander
1/2 tsp cinnamon

1 tsp cayenne pepper
2 cups red lentils, uncooked
8 cups vegetable or chicken stock
1 can diced tomatoes
salt & pepper to taste
1 can coconut milk
1 lime, juiced

In a large saucepan, heat the oil and fry the onions for about 5 minutes. Add in garlic, ginger and spices, stirring for about a minute and then add in lentils, stock and tomatoes. Add salt & pepper to taste and bring to a boil.

Lower heat and let simmer at minimum heat for 20 minutes, uncovered. When the lentils come undone, add the coconut milk. Blend together to make a creamy soup. Adjust the seasoning as desired and add lime juice.

Serve with fresh cilantro and whatever makes you happy.

The Pretty Soup
from Lis

A healthy, hearty, homey soup with lentils and sweet potatoes, named for the pretty array of gold, orange, red and pink hues in your bowl.

- 1/4 cup butter
- 1 yellow onion, chopped
- 2 leeks, sliced finely
- 4 stalks of celery, minced
- 5 garlic cloves, minced
- 2 Tbsp apple cider vinegar
- 1/4 cup white wine
- 3 bay leaves
- 6 cups vegetable stock
- 1 large sweet potato, cubed
- 4 carrots, sliced
- 1 1/2 cups lentils, cooked or canned
- 2 cups kale, chopped
- 1 cup dill, chopped
- salt & pepper to taste
- pickled beets, sliced (optional)
- sour cream or plain greek yogurt (optional)

In a very large, heavy-bottom saucepan, melt butter at medium heat. Add the onion and leeks and sauté until golden brown. Add in celery and sauté another 5 minutes. Add garlic, bay leaves, cider vinegar and wine and simmer for a few minutes, scraping the sides of the pot with a spatula to release the yummy brown bits. Next, stir in vegetable stock and sweet potato and bring to boil. Cover and cook for 20-25 minutes, until sweet potato softens.

After, use a potato masher to break down the sweet potato until it is partially blended in with the broth, creating a thicker consistency. Smaller chunks will remain. It is meant to be a thick, chunky soup. If a significant amount of water has boiled away at this point, feel free to add 1 or 2 cups of boiling water to maintain the original liquid levels (I keep a kettle of boiling water handy throughout the process). Now stir in carrots and simmer for 20 minutes or until the carrots become tender but remain firm. Add in lentils and chopped kale. Simmer for an additional 5-10 minutes or until kale is wilted. Finally, add in the dill and salt & pepper to taste, stirring everything together.

Garnish individual servings with either pickled beets or sour cream and enjoy!

What's the Dilly Pickle Soup

from Peter

A traditional Polish comfort. Make sure you only use sour dill pickles in brine for this *— Important!* recipe. Easily found at delis, or in the refrigerated deli section at the supermarket. If vinegar is in the ingredient list, then it's not brine.

1 Tbsp butter
3 garlic cloves, minced
3 allspice grains
6 cups chicken broth ← *moRRo uses veggie broth*
2 carrots, diced
1 celery stalk, chopped
1 parsnip, diced

2 potatoes, diced
2 bay leaves
4-6 dill pickles, shredded
pickle brine for sourness
salt & pepper to taste
½ cup of sour cream
1 bunch fresh dill, chopped for garnish

Melt butter over low heat in a big soup pot. Add garlic and allspice and sweat for two minutes until garlic is soft but not mushy.

Add the chicken stock to soup pot and bring to a boil. While boiling, add carrots, celery, parsnip, potatoes, bay leaves and turn down to a simmer. Cook for 10 minutes, or until veggies are soft.

Add in shredded pickles and a few tablespoons of pickle brine (to taste – the more you add, the more sour the soup will taste). Remove bay leaves and top with salt & pepper as desired. Serve hot and garnish with a generous dollop of sour cream and lots of fresh dill.

Variations:
Like it creamy? Temper your sour cream by ladling some hot soup into it first while whisking. Take the pot off the heat and stir the sour cream right into the soup.
Feeling adventurous? Make your own stock for this soup with turkey wing and veal, or a stock of smoked ribs as the Polish do. Whichever you try, shred the meat and leave in the soup to serve.

OR with vegetables as the vegetarians do.

Hello Pickles We meet again.

118

Oodles of Noodles and Beans Soup
from Ramona

19 oz can Romano beans, drained
8 cups chicken or vegetable stock
1 Tbsp olive oil
1 onion, chopped
2 celery stalks, chopped
1 carrot, diced
3 garlic cloves, minced
1/4 cup parsley
1 tsp chili pepper flakes
1 large can diced tomatoes (including juice)
1 cup mini macaroni
parmesan, grated

Purée half the beans, with a 1/2 cup of stock and set aside.

In a large soup pot, add olive oil and sauté onions, celery, carrot, garlic, parsley and pepper flakes for 10 minutes or until soft. Add the bean and stock purée, tomatoes, and the rest of the whole beans and cook for 5 minutes.

Stir in the remaining stock and bring to a light boil. Add macaroni and cook for 15 minutes or until pasta is tender.

Serve with grated parmesan and a smile.

Belly Full o' Black Bean Soup
from Morro

1 glug olive oil
1 small onion, diced
2-3 carrots, chopped
2-3 parsnips, chopped
2-3 garlic cloves, smashed
2 tsp cumin
1 tsp cayenne pepper
6 cups vegetable stock
1 can black beans, rinsed and drained
sour cream or yogurt, to garnish
parsley or cilantro, to garnish

In a big pot, heat oil and sauté onions. Toss in carrots and parsnips and cook for 3-5 minutes. Then throw in your garlic and spices, sautéing for a few more minutes. Add in broth and beans and simmer, partially covered, for 40-60 minutes, until the veggies are tender.

Using a blender, purée until smooth-ish and serve. Top it with a blob of sour cream or yogurt and parsley or cilantro (if you're into that kind of soapy-tasting thing) for pretty colours.

Dearest Farmers,

I am sorry that you have to work so very hard, toiling day in and day out. I regret that you don't always make as much money as some people who wake up much later and do a lot less and get more vacation time and never get dirty. On behalf of us (all of us), I apologize for the fact that houses and subdivisions keep being built on good soil that should be saved for your farms. And yunno what? I also feel bad that you are underappreciated because without you, we would all be in really deep trouble and have nothing to eat.

So thank you for every seed you sow, every cow you feed, every plant you water.

Sending neverending high-fives and hugs,

MORRO

PS. Go tomatoes!

Drunken Mushroom Stew

from Morro and Jasp

2 Tbsp butter
2 Tbsp olive oil
5 shallots, coarsely chopped
2 carrots, chopped into rounds
1 big parsnip, chopped
2 celery stalks, chopped
5 garlic cloves, finely chopped
1-2 cups oyster mushrooms, coarsely chopped
1-2 cups cremini mushrooms, coarsely chopped
1-2 cups shiitake mushrooms, coarsely chopped
1-2 cups portabella mushrooms, sliced
1 cup white wine
1 cup sherry
1 Tbsp parsley
1 Tbsp dried thyme
1 Tbsp dried sage
2 bay leaves
5 cups mushroom stock or enough to cover the stew while cooking
(the kasha will suck some up)
1/4 cup kasha (buckwheat)
4 potatoes, peeled and cubed
salt & pepper to taste

Marry the butter and oil in a large pot over medium heat, and then add the shallots into the mix and make 'em sweat, stirring occasionally for about 8-10 minutes or until they begin to turn golden. Invite the carrots, parsnips, and celery, and sauté until they start to turn brown. Call on over the garlic and mushrooms and sauté for a few minutes until their juice is released.

Kick it up a notch by adding wine, sherry, parsley, thyme, sage and bay leaves (unless they are fresh herbs, in which case add after stock). Cook until liquid is reduced by half, about 1-3 minutes. Add stock, kasha and potatoes. Bring to a boil then reduce to low heat, partially cover and cook for 25 minutes, or until vegetables are tender. Remove bay leaves and add salt & pepper to taste. This stew is best enjoyed with your sister...

balls about that big

Doughboy Dumplings

from Ramona

1 1/2 cups flour
1 1/2 tsp baking powder
1 Tbsp butter, softened
water as needed

Mix all ingredients together in a mixing bowl. Add water to create soft, sticky dough. Spoon balls of dough into pot, making sure there is enough stew to have them partially covered. Close lid for 15 minutes as the steam will cook the boys.

Did you know: In WWI 'Doughboy' was a term for American soldiers in the army or navy used.

Enchilada Lasagna Casserole Layered Goodness
from Jasp

This is neither an enchilada nor a lasagna really, but it *is* delicious...

2 Tbsp oil
1 large onion, diced
3 garlic cloves, minced
3 chicken breasts, cut into small pieces
½ green pepper, diced
½ cup chipotle barbecue sauce
10 oz can cream of mushroom soup
2 cups old cheddar cheese, grated
2 cups Monterey jack, grated
4-5 large tortillas
1 cup salsa, divided
¼ cup breadcrumbs
paprika

Preheat oven to 325°F

In a large pan, heat oil and add the onion and garlic. Sauté for 2 minutes on medium heat and then add the chicken and green pepper. Stir-fry for about 8 minutes, or until the chicken just cooked (it's going in the oven so don't cook it too long or it will be dry, and I will take no responsibility). Add chipotle sauce, soup, 1 cup of cheddar, and 1 cup of Monterey jack. Cook until the cheese is melted and it looks like a delicious cheesy mixture and smells like yummy smoky chipotle.

Butter a large casserole dish and tear the tortilla pieces to line the bottom. Spread ½ cup of salsa on the tortilla, then pour half of the delicious cheesy chicken mixture over that. Then repeat those layers again (tortilla, salsa, cheesy-chickeny goodness) and then top it with the rest of the cheeses. Sprinkle on the breadcrumbs and some paprika so it looks pretty! Bake it for 50-60 minutes and then wait 10 minutes before eating it or you'll burn your mouth and won't be able to taste all the yummy flavours.

Serve it with sour cream and guacamole for dipping and maximum deliciousness.

Bengali-Style Chicken Curry
from Mrs. Roy

- 1 Tbsp canola or sunflower oil
- ½ tsp cumin seeds
- 3" piece cinnamon bark, broken in two
- 2 cardamom pods, mushed
- 1 medium red onion, diced
- 3 garlic cloves, minced
- 2 chicken breasts, cubed
- ½ -1 tsp turmeric
- ½ -1 tsp dhana jeera
- ½ -1 tsp fresh ginger, grated
- 2 pinches crushed chili flakes
- 3 pinches salt, divided
- 3 pinches sugar, divided
- 2 tomatoes, diced
- 2 pinches black pepper
- ½ cup plain yogurt

Pour oil into a large pan over low-medium heat. Add cumin seeds, cinnamon stick and cardamom pods to oil. Then add onion into the pan with the garlic. Sauté over low-medium heat until onion is transparent, then add in chicken.

When chicken is a third of the way cooked, add turmeric, dhana jeera, ginger and crushed chili flakes. Next, add 2 pinches of salt and sugar and all the tomatoes. Stir the chicken curry, and let it have a good time while you simmer it for 7 minutes. Add a little bit of warm water. Cook over low-medium heat until the water evaporates and you have a thick curry - about 10 minutes. Smell checks are important along the way to make sure the spices are blending nicely.

While the chicken is simmering, mix the yogurt with 1 pinch of sugar, salt and the pepper. Add ¼ cup of water and beat together until it is very smooth. Then add some of the warm curry sauce into the yogurt mixture to temper it. If you don't do this, the yogurt will separate when added to the chicken. Then slowly mix the yogurt into the curry. Let it cook for a few more minutes and then remove from heat and serve with basmati rice.

Serve your rice with a rice hand. It's traditional and it tastes better ...or at least we think so.

Chana My-Sala
from Anusree

1 Tbsp sunflower or canola oil
1 1/2 cups white onion, diced
2 garlic cloves, minced
1/2 tsp fresh ginger, grated
28 oz can chickpeas with juice, divided
1 tsp turmeric
1 pinch sugar

3 pinches salt, divided
1 tsp dhana jeera
1 tsp chana masala seasoning
1 red bell pepper, diced
1/2 tsp garam masala
1/4 cup warm water

Pour oil into a pot over medium heat, and once it heats up, add onions, sautéing them until they are translucent. Stir in garlic and ginger. Drain 1/2 cup chickpea juice from can and set aside. Pour remainder of juice and chickpeas in, mix and cover for 2 minutes. Add turmeric, dhana jeera, a pinch of salt and a pinch of sugar.

Cover and simmer for 2 more minutes then add chana seasoning and red peppers. Add the rest of the chickpea juice when it starts to get dry. Then add garam masala and stir. Add 1/4 cup warm water and cover for 8 minutes. Add 2 more pinches of salt. Enjoy with rice.

Southern Cheese Grits
from Chef Thess at Southern Accent

5 cups water
1 cup grits, medium stone ground
2 Tbsp butter
2 1/8 cup milk
1/4 cup olive oil
1/2 cup onions, chopped
1/4 cup celery, chopped
1/4 cup red pepper, chopped

1 jalapeño, seeded and chopped
1 head garlic, roasted
2 tsp salt
1 tsp black pepper, ground
1/4 cup parsley, finely chopped
1/2 cup cheddar cheese, shredded and divided
2 eggs, lightly beaten

Bring water to a boil, slowly add grits, stirring constantly. Reduce heat to low, cover pan and simmer grits for 30 minutes. Remove from heat and add butter and milk.

Preheat oven to 350°F

In a saucepan, heat oil and add onions, cooking until golden brown. Then add celery, jalapeño and red pepper, cook until transparent and add roasted garlic. Add salt and black pepper. Cool down and in a big bowl, mix grits mixture with parsley, eggs, vegetables, and 1/4 cup of the cheddar cheese.

Pour the mixture into a greased pan, sprinkle the rest of the cheese on and cook in the oven until the top browns, about 15-20 minutes.

Cod au Gratin
(pronounced "cod-a grat-in")
from Ramona

4 cups cod, cooked
2 cups milk
4 Tbsp flour
1/2 tsp salt
1/8 tsp pepper (white pepper if you have it)
1 cup white cheese (grated mozzarella)
1/2 cup ricotta

Preheat oven to 300°F

Once cooked, flake the fish into chunks. In a saucepan, mix the milk with the flour, salt and pepper to make a white sauce. Whisk constantly so it doesn't burn and until it gets thick. You can add a splash of white wine to the sauce for an extra kick if you want. Mix the cheeses into the white sauce. Arrange the chunks of fish in a really well buttered casserole dish, and then pour the cheese sauce over the fish. Bake for 25 minutes.

To cook the cod put it in the oven or fry it up in a pan for 10-15 min until it's flaky.

Better Than Your Mom's Lasagna
from Ms. R.M. Green

24 oz container cottage cheese
1 small container ricotta cheese
2 eggs
1 large onion, diced
½ cup celery, diced
4 garlic cloves, diced
1 Tbsp butter
1 red bell pepper, diced
1 green bell pepper, diced
1½ lbs of extra lean ground beef
28 oz can diced tomatoes

for a veggie option leave out the beef

32 oz can tomato sauce (your favourite kind)
1 small can tomato paste
2 Tbsp oregano
¼ cup parsley
2 Tbsp basil
1 Tbsp of hot pepper flakes (or more if you like spicy foods)
1 package lasagna noodles
2 cups of mozzarella cheese, grated
1 cup of mushrooms, sliced
2 cups spinach, ripped into pieces

Preheat oven to 375°F

Mix cottage cheese, ricotta and eggs together in a small bowl and put to the side.

In a large pot, sauté onions, celery and garlic in butter. Make sure not to burn the garlic or it will turn bitter. Once the onions turn clear-ish, add peppers and beef. Cook on medium-low heat until the beef is browned. Add diced tomatoes, tomato sauce, tomato paste and spices. That's the sauce!

In another large pot, cook the lasagna noodles for about half the cooking time given on the package. If it says cook for 10 minutes, cook for 5; if it says cook for 15 minutes cook for about 10. Once the pasta is par cooked, line the bottom of a large casserole dish with your sauce mixture. Then add a layer of noodles. Layer the cheese and egg mixture on top and sprinkle with 1 cup of mozzarella cheese. Add another layer of noodles and another layer of sauce. Then add a layer of sliced mushrooms and a layer of spinach. Or the other way around. Or both at the same time – whatever you want! Top with more noodles, more sauce, and the rest of the mozzarella cheese. Cover with tin foil (tent it over so it's not touching the cheese if possible) and bake for 45 minutes. Remove foil and bake for another 15 minutes until edges are golden.

We like to use the same sauce recipe for spaghetti OR if you add chili powder and kidney beans it becomes a yummy chili. YUM!

Just one of them days
by MORRO

Today I am feeling kinda blue.
No particular reason that I can think of
except that some things are askewwww.
My porridge is a little too goopy,
and I'm just a little droopy,
the grass it is too long,
everyone I talk to seems a wee bit wrong.
The sky is grey like putty,
the birds all sound sorta grunty.
I sure don't want to do my hair.
On a day like today I want to sit and stare.
So thanks for the tea, no offense but it just
   made me have to pee.
All I need from you on a day when I feel like
   a lug,
is nothing more than a simple HUG.

Lazy Dayzy

When you've got nowhere to go, no place to be, no particular location that requires your presence. You got to sleep in. There's a few chores, but you can do them later. You just wanna slow down and smell the sweet sweet syrup. And who knows maybe you'll order pizza later ... maybe not.

us sleeping

Maple Squash Pancakes

Chez Shea Oven Pancake

Apple of My Eye Pancake

Toast

Thrice Cooked Brekkie Taters

Grilled Cheese French Toast with Butter Rum Pears

'You Say Potato, I Say Potato' Potato Egg Tart

Turkey Lurkey Quiche

Quinoa Crust

100% Canadian Maple Baked Beaners

Jal & Ched Cornbread

Cinnamony Sugary Quick Bread

We Be Chillin' With Fro Yo

Maple Squash Pancakes

from Morro and Jasp

1¾ cups quinoa flour
¼ cup brown sugar, packed
2 tsp baking powder
1 tsp baking soda
1 tsp cinnamon
1 tsp ground ginger
½ tsp ground nutmeg
½ tsp ground cloves
½ tsp salt
1¾ cups buttermilk
¼ cup maple syrup
1 cup cooked squash, puréed
(acorn or butternut are yummiest!)
2 large eggs
2 Tbsp veg oil
asiago or parmesan, crumbled (optional)
apples, cut into tiny chunks (optional)
pepper, ground (optional)

In a big ol' bowl, mix up the flour, sugar, baking powder, baking soda, cinnamon, ginger, nutmeg, cloves and salt.

In another bowl, whisk together buttermilk, syrup, squash purée, eggs, and oil. Pour the wet ingredients into the dry ingredients and mix until just blended. Here's where you can add a sneaky and delicious mixin', like cheese, apples, or pepper if you want. But these pancakes are also super yummy on their own.

Scoop spoonfuls of batter onto a greased frying pan at medium heat and make a circle, or a blob, or whatever shape makes you feel warm and toasty on the inside. When it starts to bubble a bit, flip it on the other side and cook a little more. Serve with syrup, nuts, whipped cream or whatever tickles your pancake fancy.

We like to double this recipe because it is so good that we always want seconds... thirds... fourths.

Chez Shea Oven Pancake
from Seamus and Fiona

2 eggs
1½ Tbsp sugar
½ tsp salt (optional)
½ cup flour
2 Tbsp butter, melted
1⅓ cup milk
cinnamon & sugar to sprinkle (optional)

Preheat oven to 400°F

In a bowl, beat eggs and sugar until fluffy. Stir in salt, flour, and melted butter. Gradually add milk and keep beating. Pour batter into a buttered 8x8" oven safe dish. Bake for 30 minutes or until soft but not runny. Sprinkle with cinnamon and sugar. Cut into pieces and serve with your favourite fresh fruit or fruit preserves.

mmm!   -mmm!

Apple of My Eye Pancake
from Frederick

Batter:
4 large eggs
1 cup milk
1 cup flour
1/2 tsp salt
2 Tbsp butter

Filling:
1 1/4 lbs apples
1/3 cup butter
1/3 cup sugar
cinnamon to taste
nutmeg to taste

Preheat oven to 450°F

Beat eggs, milk, flour and salt until it is a smooth batter. Melt butter to coat a 12" skillet or 9x13" casserole dish. Heat up the dish in the oven until it's hot, then remove it and pour the batter in. Bake it for 15 minutes, then remove it and pierce the bubbles in the batter. Lower the oven temperature to 350°F and bake for another for 10 minutes. That's your pancake!

To make the filling, peel and thinly slice apples and sauté them in butter. Add sugar and season to taste with cinnamon and nutmeg. Cook on medium heat for 8-10 minutes until tender, but not mushy. Pour the filling into the cooked pancake. Cut into squares and serve!

Toast
from Jasp

1 piece of bread
butter (optional)
jam (optional)
peanut butter (optional)
cinnamon sugar (optional)

Take a piece of bread. Put it in the toaster and press the lever down. Wait for it to pop up - time may vary on different toasters. Once you hear the pop, the bread has transformed into toast. Stare at the toast and decide if you have energy to put on a topping. If you do, put it on. If you don't, just eat the toast naked. Ladies and gentlemen, toast.

Thrice Cooked Brekkie Taters
from The Sir

2 baking potatoes, chopped into cubes
2 yellow potatoes, chopped into cubes
2 red potatoes, chopped into cubes
½ cup olive oil
steak spice

Preheat oven to 400°F

Boil a pot of water and throw in the potatoes. Boil the potatoes for 5-7 minutes so they are par-cooked and still firm. Drain them well. Heat ¼ cup oil in a large skillet or frying pan, adding potatoes when oil is heated.

Add 3 shakes of steak spice, making sure to coat potatoes. Cook over medium-high heat for 10 minutes, or until potatoes are almost fully cooked.

On a large cookie sheet, add remaining oil and potatoes and place in the oven for 15 minutes or until the corners are crispy and the potatoes are cooked all the way through. Remove from oven, add 2 more shakes of steak spice and let sit for 2 minutes before serving.

> Perfect to go with a leisurly ~~breakfast~~ brunch after you got to sleep in.

Especially nice when your sister makes them for you so you can sleep even more. ♡

Grilled Cheese French Toast with Butter Rum Pears
from Morro and Jasp

3 eggs
1 tsp vanilla extract
3 Tbsp butter, divided
8 slices fresh raisin bread
2 Tbsp brown sugar

pinch of cinnamon
4 pears, thinly sliced
1-2 oz rum
pinch of salt
1 cup old cheddar cheese, grated

♡ A Perfect Recipe for a Special Brunch

Preheat oven to 400°F

Whisk together eggs and vanilla in a bowl. Heat 1 Tbsp of butter in a large frying pan over medium heat. Dunk bread into egg mixture and fry in pan. Repeat until all 8 pieces of toast are Frenched.

In a separate frying pan, add remaining 2 Tbsp of butter with brown sugar, and cinnamon. Melt over medium heat, making sure all ingredients are blended. Add sliced pears and rum. Cook until pear slices are soft but still whole. Add salt towards the end.

Sprinkle cheese between 2 pieces of French toast to make sandwiches. Put the sandwiches on a cookie sheet and bake for 5 minutes or until cheese is melted. Remove from oven, top with pears and serve. Mmmm...boozy breakfast.

'You Say Potato, I Say Potato' Egg Tart
from Morro

6 potatoes, peeled
2-4 glugs olive oil, divided
2 garlic cloves, crushed
1 big handful spinach
1 cup ricotta cheese

5 eggs, beaten
2 tsp lemon peel, grated
3/4 cup old cheddar cheese
salt & pepper to taste
1 red pepper, sliced

Preheat oven to 350°F

Slice the taters so they are thin – like the thickness of your earlobe. Warm up 1 glug of oil in a big frying pan and line the pan with as many tater pieces as you can fit and cook 'em up for a couple minutes on each side, or until they're tender and golden. When they're done, put them on a plate and continue to cook the rest of the tater pieces.

Cook the garlic in 1 glug of oil, for about 1 minute, until the yummy smells start to waft up to your nose. Add the spinach and cook it with a lid until it just begins to wilt. Drain out any liquid and put the cooked spinach and garlic in a bowl and toss in ricotta, half of the cheddar, eggs, and lemon zest. Stir it all up, and add salt & pepper to taste.

Now it's time to put your tart together. Grease a large pie plate and arrange the cooked taters all along the inside and the sides, leaving no spot uncovered! Scoop in the spinach mixture and arrange red peppers on top in a pretty design. Sprinkle the rest of the cheddar on top. Bake it for 50-60 minutes or until the egg is no longer runny. Cut it into slices and serve it up!

Turkey Lurkey Quiche
from Kristy, Christine, Steven, Otto and the whole family!

1 cup cooked turkey, cubed
1 cup celery, chopped
1 Tbsp onion, minced
3 eggs, beaten
1 cup cheddar cheese, grated
¼ cup mayonnaise
2 tsp mustard
paprika

Preheat oven to 375°F

Mix everything together and place in a prepared pie crust (one of our favourites is below!) sprinkle with paprika and bake for 40-45 minutes.

Quinoa Crust
from Morro and Jasp

½ cup quinoa, rinsed
1 cup water
1 egg
¼ cup parmesan, grated

Preheat oven to 375°F

Bring the quinoa and water to a boil, reduce the heat, and simmer covered, for about 15 minutes, or until most of the water has been absorbed and the quinoa is tender. Let it sit covered for 5 minutes.

Mix the quinoa, egg and parmesan together and press into the bottom of a greased pie plate. Then pour in your filling and bake for 40-45 minutes.

100% Canadian Maple Baked Beaners
from Morro and Jasp

1 lb dry red kidney beans
8 cups water
1 large yellow onion, diced
1 bay leaf
6 whole black peppercorns
3/4 cup pure maple syrup
1/2 cup brown sugar, lightly packed
1/2 cup ketchup
1 Tbsp chili paste
1 Tbsp fresh ginger, grated
1 tsp salt

*We make this on a cool fall day with a warm loaf of bread.

Put the beaners in a bowl. Cover them with water and refrigerate overnight.

Drain the beaners and put them in a big pot with water, onion, bay leaf, and peppercorns. Bring it all to a boil then lower the heat and simmer it for about 45 minutes, or until the beaners get tender. Drain the beaners, keeping the cooking liquid for later.

Preheat oven to 225°F

In a large saucepan, whisk together maple syrup, brown sugar, ketchup, chili paste, ginger, salt and 1 1/2 cups of the cooking liquid from the beans. Bring to a simmer and cook over low heat for about 6 minutes.

Move the beaners to a Dutch oven or bean pot and add the maple syrup sauce. Cover with the lid and bake for 6-8 hours checking in on them every now and then. If beaners get too dry add 1/2 cup more of the cooking liquid. Take away the lid for last 30 minutes to thicken sauce.

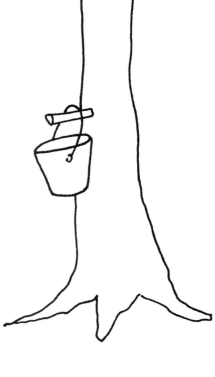

Jal & Ched Cornbread
from Morro and Jasp

3 cups flour
1 cup yellow cornmeal
¼ cup sugar
2 Tbsp baking powder
2 tsp salt
2 cups milk
3 large eggs, lightly beaten
½ lb unsalted butter, melted
2 cups sharp cheddar, grated and divided
⅓ cup green onions, chopped – plus more
3 Tbsp fresh jalapeño peppers, seeded and minced (about 2-3 peppers)

Preheat oven to 350°F

In a big bowl, mix up your flour, cornmeal, sugar, baking powder and salt.

In another bowl, slosh together milk, eggs and butter. Pour the wet ingredients into the dry stuff and mix it all up with a wooden spoon until most of the lumps are no more – but don't overmix it, you rigorous, vigorous chef, you!

Plop in the grated cheddar, the onions (saving a little bit of both to sprinkle on top) and the jalapeños and mix it all up. Leave it alone for 20 minutes. Don't even think about putting it in the fridge or eating it raw. Just let it be.

Grease a 9x13" baking pan. Pour the batter inside, and sprinkle with remaining cheese and bits of onion. Bake it for 30-35 minutes, then do the toothpick test. Let it cool down a bit and cut it up. You can eat it warm or cool, depending on how you feel that day.

Did you know First Nations peoples were using ground corn to make bread waaay before European settlers 'discovered' it?

Cornbread is also sometimes referred to as 'Johnny Cakes' and 'Hushpuppies'!

Cinnamony Sugary Quick Bread
from Cylus

1 1/3 cups white sugar, divided
2 cups flour
1/2 tsp salt
1 Tbsp baking powder
1 egg, beaten

1 cup milk
1/3 cup vegetable oil
2 tsp cinnamon, divided
1 Tbsp brown sugar

Preheat oven to 350°F

Mix 1 cup of the white sugar with the flour, salt and baking powder in a large bowl. In another bowl, mix egg, milk and oil together. Add the wet ingredients to the dry ingredients and stir until moist. Pour half the mixture into a greased 9x5" pan. Sprinkle with 1 tsp cinnamon and remaining white sugar. Pour the other half of the mixture on top. Sprinkle brown sugar and remaining cinnamon over the top. Bake for 45-50 minutes. Let stand for 10 minutes before removing from the pan and then cool on a wire rack.

"Wait don't go!"

Hey, did you know that quick bread is a type of bread that uses something other than yeast to rise.

The World's Best Frozen Yogurt
from Jasp

Using your favourite search engine, surf the interwebs to find a frozen yogurt place close to you. (Make sure to check their hours, 'cuz if you got a late night craving and you go all the way there and then it's closed, you're gonna be mad.) Alternatively, you can use something called a "phone book." I think I used to sit on one during meals in restaurants when I was young or something...

Having found your destination, place approximately $5 in your pocket (more if you are one of those "gotta try everything" types) and then select your mode of transportation based on availability and ability. Some popular choices are driving, subway, streetcar, bus, bike, skateboard and spaceship. I usually just walk though.

Once you arrive, make sure to sample each and every flavour. (You may have to try some flavours more than once for this step). If, for some reason, you've wound up in one of those places that don't offer samples, begin again from the search engine stage.

Using the serving bowl provided, dispense a large swirl of your two favourite flavours. Add toffee bits, roasted coconut, cherries, strawberries, 2 brownie pieces, and chocolate and/or peanut butter sauce over your frozen yogurt (you can use any toppings, but I highly recommend this combination).

All you have to do is have the cashier weigh your bowl and pay for your yogurt (this is where the $5 comes in). Finally, enjoy The World's Best Frozen Yogurt and be proud of yourself.

Note: This dish is best served on a patio on a hot summer evening with someone special, though make sure they brought their own $5 or be willing to pay for theirs 'cuz once you taste this, you're not gonna want to share!

NOSTALGIC

When you long for the good ol' times when you sat on Grandma's lap while she showed you old photos and told you stories about walking to school uphill both ways, and who used to live in the little green house down the lane, and when they used to churn butter by hand, and how she fell in love... all the while delicious smells wafted out of her kitchen.

A+ Applesauce

Blueberry Buckle

Harriet's Magical Spice Cake

Banana-Nana Bread

Save the Date Squares

Slow as Molasses Buns

Pat's Shortbread Cookies

Crispy Oatmeal Cookies

In a Ginger Snap

Sweet Raspberry Cupcakes

Half Pennies

Good Ol' Carrot Pineapple Muffins

Mary's Mustard Relish

The Infamous Green Jello Mould 'Salad'

Super Fun Marshmallow 'Salad'

↑ moRRo ↵
— 11 YRS   wont fit
             on chart
— moRRo   anymoRe.
—← 10 YRS

Jasp —
14 yrs — 9 YRS
13 yrs =
12 yrs — 8 YRS
11 yrs =← 7 YRS
10 yrs —
9 yrs — 6 YRS
7+8 —↙
7 yrs →= ←5 YRS
6 yrs —
5 yrs →— 4 YRS
4 yrs ↘
3 yrs ↘ -← 3 YRS
2 yrs ↘= → 2 YRS

Jasp →- ← moRRo 1 YRS
1 yr old —

Dear Gramma,

thanks for having us over to your house and letting us pet Mooshy. She didn't even scratch us once.

And remember those chocolate wafer coookies you gave us. And the juicy peaches you picked right off the tree? AND that fizzy ginger drink? those were all really yummy. And we loved the story about the family of bears that went on a picnic by the Lake and ate pickles.

Can we come over again soon?

We love you!

MoRRo + JasP@

morro; Jasp age 5 and 6½.

A+ Applesauce
from Sheila

My Mom used to make the best applesauce.
It started with the ingredients.
My aunt Ruby and uncle Ralph had an apple orchard. We would go and pick "grounders" for fifty cents a bushel. Mostly they were Macintosh apples. They were the best apples - so juicy and full of flavour, both sweet and tart at the same time. I came to the conclusion that these were the apples that the tree deemed ripe and let go of. They would be only lightly bruised, as there was long grass under the trees.
The whole apples were quartered and put into a big pot and just covered with water.
This was brought to a boil and then simmered until the apples were soft.
My mom had a big funnel-shaped colander that would sit over a large bowl.
There was a wedge-shaped press, perhaps called a pestle that echoed the shape of the colander.
The apples were pressed through the colander so the seeds and skins were strained off.
A small bit of dark brown sugar was then added, although the apples were so sweet it was not always necessary. And sometimes she would sprinkle cinnamon on the top too.
And that's all there was to making my Mom's applesauce.

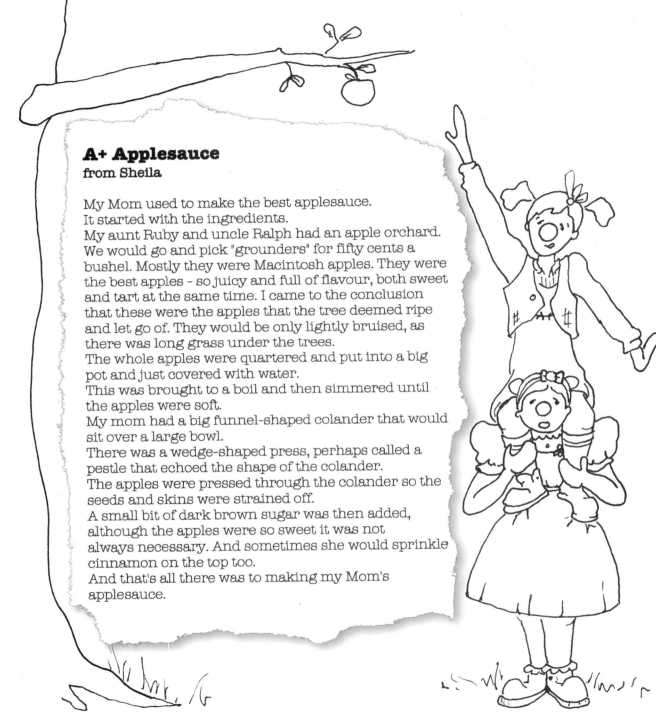

Blueberry Buckle
from Granny Bernice

2 cups wild blueberries, fresh or thawed
½ cup sugar
1 Tbsp cornstarch
½ lemon, juiced
½ cup butter, softened
½ cup sugar
1 egg
1½ cups flour
2 tsp baking powder
½ tsp salt
1 cup milk

Preheat oven to 350°F

In a glass baking dish, combine blueberries, sugar, cornstarch and lemon juice. Then add enough water so that the berries are almost covered and set aside.

In a mixing bowl, cream butter, then add sugar, then stir in egg. In another bowl, mix the flour, baking powder and salt together. Add the dry ingredients into the wet, alternating with milk. Beat until smooth and spread over berry mixture. Bake for 50 minutes. Serve hot or cold.

Note: You can cook the berry mixture first without the cornstarch and then add the topping.

You can also sub raspberries, strawberries or a mixture of berries.

Harriet's Magical Spice Cake
from Nana Harriet

The dry stuff:
1 1/2 cups flour
1/2 cup sugar
1 tsp cinnamon
3/4 tsp ground cloves
1/2 tsp ground ginger
1/2 tsp ground nutmeg
1 tsp baking soda
1/2 tsp salt

The wet stuff:
6 Tbsp canola or corn oil
1 Tbsp vinegar
1 tsp almond extract
1 cup cold water

that's our friend → Harriet

Order of business:

Preheat the oven to 350°F

Get out a cake pan. (8x8" or close to it.) Don't grease it. Geez.
Sift all the dry stuff into the cake pan. Or just bung it in.
Stir it up some. Make three holes in the dry mix: a large, a medium and a small. Like the 3 bears.
Pour the oil into the large hole. Ta da!
Pour the vinegar into the medium hole. Ta da!
Pour the almond extract into the small hole. Ta da!
Say "Abracadabra." Watch the vinegar hole get frothy.
Pour the water over the whole kit and kaboodle. Take a fork and mix it all up.
Bung it in the oven to bake it. It'll be 20 minutes or so, maybe 25. Stick it with a toothpick to see if anything sticks.
Let it cool a few minutes before you flip it onto a cooling rack. When it's cool, slather it up with icing. Makes 9 servings if you're dainty about it. Makes 6 servings if you're not. Pig.

Harriet's Almond Icing

Soften up about 1/4 cup of butter
Add about 3/4 cup of icing sugar
Add a few Tbsp of something creamy. Like cream. Or milk. To soften it if you need to. Otherwise, skip it.
Add a dollop of almond butter (up to you. My dollop is about 1 1/2 tsp)
Add a swish of pure almond extract (up to you. My swish is about 1/2 tsp)

Note: If your spices are more than 2 yrs old, chuck'em, ya pack rat... Fresh spices will give a more robust taste. If you don't want to chuck 'em, then double the amount.

Banana-Nana Bread
from Grandmother Green

- 1/2 cup milk
- 1/2 cup water
- 1 tbsp vinegar
- 4 cups flour
- 1 tsp baking powder
- 1 tsp baking soda
- 1/2 tsp salt
- 1/2 tsp nutmeg
- 1/2 cup butter
- 1 1/2 cups sugar
- 2 eggs
- 3 bananas, mashed
- 1/2 cup walnuts, chopped (optional)

Preheat oven to 350°F

In a small mixing bowl, combine milk, water, and vinegar and set aside. In a medium mixing bowl, combine the flour, baking powder, baking soda, salt and nutmeg together and set aside. In large mixing bowl, cream the butter and sugar together and then add in the eggs. Beat until light and fluffy and then add in pre-mashed bananas.

Alternating the wet and dry mixtures, add these to the creamed mixture, stirring in walnuts, if you want. Pour into a well greased and floured bundt pan. Bake for 1 hour and 15 minutes. Or pour into 2 loaf pans and bake for 1 hour.

your tone is rather unappeeling morro

Save the Date Squares
from Grandmother White

Filling:
2 cups dates
1/2 cup sugar
1 cup water
1 Tbsp lemon juice

Crumb:
1 1/2 cups flour
1/2 tsp baking soda
1/4 tsp baking powder
1 3/4 cups oats
1 cup brown sugar
3/4 cup butter

Preheat oven to 375°F

Combine filling ingredients in a pot and simmer until thick, stirring and being careful not to burn the mixture. Let cool.

In a large bowl, combine flour, baking soda, baking powder and stir, adding in oats, and brown sugar. Work in the butter with your fingertips.

Pat half of the crumb mixture in the bottom of a lightly greased 9" pan. Spread the filling overtop and sprinkle the remaining oat mixture on top. Bake for 45 minutes or until golden brown. Cool and cut into squares.

Slow as Molasses Buns
from Grandmother White

½ cup butter
1 cup sugar
1 cup fancy molasses
1 cup boiling water
1 tsp ground cloves

2 tsp ground all spice
2 tsp ground ginger
4 tsp baking soda
5½ cups flour

Preheat oven to 350°F

Cream butter in a mixing bowl, then add sugar and cream with butter. Next, add molasses and boiling water and stir. Mix in spices and baking soda, and then gradually mix in flour until combined. Chill for 20 minutes and then shape into buns by rolling out the dough ½ - 1" thick and cutting it into circles with the rim of a drinking glass. Or for a more rustic look, drop a Tbsp sized blob of dough onto a greased cookie sheet. Bake for 15-20 minutes or until firm.

Pat's Shortbread Cookies
from Grandma Pat

1 cup butter
1/2 cup icing sugar

1/2 cup corn starch
1 cup flour

Preheat oven to 300°F

Leave butter at room temperature for 3 hours. Sift flour, sugar and corn starch together twice. Add to softened butter and mix well. Chill dough for 30 minutes. Form into small balls and flatten with a fork. Bake for 20-25 minutes.

add a piece of dried cherry on top each for a pretty touch ♡

Crispy Oatmeal Cookies
from Grandma Pat

1/2 tsp baking soda
4 Tbsp hot water
1 1/2 cups flour
1 1/2 cups minute oats

1 cup sugar
1/2 tsp salt
1 cup butter

Preheat oven to 350°F

Stir baking soda into hot water. Mix everything together and make small balls. Press them flat. Bake for 10-12 minutes in greased pan. Remove from pan while warm.

In a Ginger Snap
from Grandma Pat

3/4 cup shortening
1 cup sugar
1 egg
4 Tbsp molasses
2 cups flour
2 tsp baking powder

2 tsp baking soda
1 tsp salt
1 tsp cinnamon
1 tsp ground cloves
1 tsp ground ginger

Preheat oven to 350°F

Mix everything together. Make into small balls and flatten. Bake on a greased cookie sheet for 8-12 minutes.

Sweet Raspberry Cupcakes
from Grandma Lee

Batter:
1 2/3 cups sifted flour
3 tsp baking powder
1 tsp salt
1/2 cup shortening
1 cup sugar
2 eggs
1 tsp lemon rind, grated
2/3 cup milk
1/2 tsp vanilla extract
1 cup raspberries

Icing:
1/2 cup salted butter
2 tsp lemon juice
2 Tbsp raspberries, crushed
4 cups icing sugar, sifted
2 Tbsp milk

Preheat oven to 375°F

To make the batter, sift flour with baking powder and salt.

In a separate bowl, cream shortening until light, gradually adding sugar until light and fluffy. Add eggs one at a time, beating well between each addition. Stir in rind. In another bowl, combine milk and vanilla. Add dry ingredients to creamed mixture, alternating with milk, combining lightly after each addition. Fold in raspberries.

Pour 2/3 full into a greased or papered muffin tin, or mini muffin tin if you want more to go around! Bake for 20-25 minutes.

To make the icing, cream butter until light. Blend in lemon juice and raspberries. Gradually add icing sugar, alternate with milk. Beat until of spreading consistency.

Spread the icing on top of the cupcakes et voila!

Like cheesie shortbread

Half Pennies
from Grandma Parrish

2 cups cheddar cheese, grated
½ cup butter
1 cup flour
3 Tbsp onion soup mix

Preheat oven to 350°F

Knead all ingredients together well and roll into a log. Wrap and chill overnight. Slice into ¼" thick pieces and bake on an ungreased pan for 10-15 minutes.

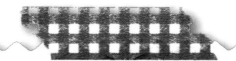

Good Ol' Carrot Pineapple Muffins
from Grandma Pat

1½ cups flour
1 tsp baking powder
1 tsp cinnamon
½ tsp salt
1 tsp baking soda
1 tsp nutmeg

1 cup sugar
1 cup carrots, grated
½ cup pineapple, crushed and drained
1 tsp vanilla extract
⅔ cup vegetable oil
2 eggs

Preheat oven to 350°F

Sift together dry ingredients in a bowl. In another bowl, mix together carrots, pineapple, vanilla, oil and eggs. Slowly add and blend the wet mixture into the dry mixture. Beat it all together for 2 minutes, or until well blended. Grease muffin tins or add muffin papers and fill ½ full. Bake for 20 minutes.

Mary's Mustard Relish
from Grannie Mary

5½ cups cauliflower, chopped
1½ cups small pickling onions, chopped
7 cups pickling cucumbers, chopped
2 cups water
½ cup salt
4 cups white vinegar

1 cup flour
4 Tbsp dry mustard
4 cups sugar
1 Tbsp turmeric
2½ cups green and red bell peppers, chopped

In a large container, soak cauliflower, onions and cucumbers in water and salt overnight.

The next day, combine vinegar, flour, mustard, sugar and turmeric in a large pot and bring to a boil, making sure sauce doesn't thicken too much.

Remove vegetables from salt water and rinse to remove some of the salt. Mix rinsed vegetables with bell peppers and sauce.

Scoop the relish into sterilized jars and seal in a water bath.

✷ make sure you go online or learn from a beloved elder how to safely sterilize and seal jars if you are canning.

If you want to jar this you'll need 6 250ml canning jars.

The Infamous Green Jello Mould 'Salad'
from Grandma Annis

1 package green gelatin
1 cup hot water
½ cup cold water
8 oz cream cheese, softened

Mix gelatin powder in hot water. Once it's dissolved, stir in the cold water. Whip the cream cheese and gradually add the prepared gelatin with a hand blender. Mix and pour into jello mould, or any fun shaped ring pan. Put in the fridge and let it set.

To remove from mould, set it in warm water quickly to loosen it. Place a plate on top of mould, flip to empty and put back in the fridge to set again for at least an hour.

Variation: For an orange version, use orange gelatin and mix in grated carrots and chopped pineapple before setting in the fridge.

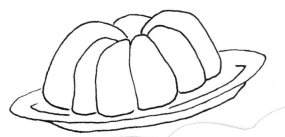

Our favourite colourful additions to a big family dinner. Only Grandma could make dinner this fun.

Super Fun Marshmallow 'Salad'
from Grandma Lee

2 eggs, beaten
2 Tbsp vinegar
4 Tbsp sugar
2 Tbsp butter
1 cup heavy cream, whipped
2 cups mandarin oranges, drained
2 cups cherries or grapes, halved
2 cups pineapples, cubed
⅛ tsp salt
2 cups colourful mini marshmallows

Beat the eggs in the top of a double boiler. Add vinegar and sugar, beating constantly until thick and smooth. Remove from heat, add butter and cool. When mixture is cool, fold in the whipped cream, oranges, cherries or grapes, pineapple, salt and marshmallows.

Chill for 24 hours and serve to happy, happy children – and grown-ups who secretly love it just as much as the kids!

Festive

When you want to enjoy some holiday yummies anytime of the year... even if it's not a holiday... even if it's not your holiday.... even if you hate holidays...

good luck surviving the holidays ➢

Classical Gingerbreads

Loyal Royal Icing

Festive Fruitcake

CANberry Orange Chocolate Rounds

Lucky Latkes

Yorkshire Pudding

Secret Stuffing

More More More Matzah Crunch

A Brisket A Brasket

Harvest Apple Torte

Wondrous White Chocolate Biscotti

I Wish I Wish For A Mushroom Knish

Melt In Your Mouth Sugar Cookies

Holla for Challah

Classical Gingerbreads

from Morro

4 cups light brown sugar
2 Tbsp cinnamon
2 Tbsp ground ginger
2 tsp ground allspice
1 tsp ground cloves
1 Tbsp baking soda
1 cup boiling water
2 cups butter
1 cup molasses
8 cups flour

Preheat oven to 300°F

Combine brown sugar, cinnamon, ginger, allspice, cloves, and baking soda with boiling water in a large bowl and mix. Add butter and mix in until melted, then add molasses. Gradually stir in flour.

On a floured surface, roll out until dough is 1/4" thick and use your favorite cookie cutters to make fun shapes! (Sing a classical song while you do it. I highly recommend Bach.)

Bake on an ungreased cookie sheet for 10-20 minutes until cookies plump up but make sure they don't burn. Cool for 5-10 minutes before moving.

Loyal Royal Icing

from Morro

2 egg whites
2 tsp fresh lemon juice
3 cups icing sugar

Beat eggs whites in a small bowl with lemon juice. Add sugar and continue to beat until smooth. Use immediately to draw faces and clothes on your gingerbread people so they're not cold! Store in an airtight container if you don't use it all up (or eat it all up) right away!

Festive Fruitcake
from Grandmother Green

A highly coveted and secret recipe...

2 1/2 cups flour
1 tsp cinnamon
1 tsp ground allspice
1 tsp ground mace
1 tsp ground nutmeg
1 tsp ground ginger
1/4 tsp ground cloves
1 lb glazed cherries, halved
1 lb raisins
8 oz mix fruit
1 lb dates, cut into pieces

4 cups walnuts
1 cup butter
1 1/2 cups brown sugar
4 eggs
2 tsp lemon juice
2 tsp vanilla extract
2 tsp maple extract
1 tsp baking soda (add to 1/4 cup warm water)
1 large mug Big Dipper rum

The sticky glazed kind for baking you can get at the bulk store → (pointing to glazed cherries)

about 3/4 cup of dark rum → (pointing to Big Dipper rum)

Combine dry ingredients. Add 1/2 cup of dry mixture to cherries, raisins, mix fruit, and dates. Then add 1/2 cup of dry mixture to walnuts. Put the rest of the dry ingredients aside. Let sit overnight. (It will help them not sink in the cake).

Preheat oven to 250°F

Cream butter, adding sugar, eggs, lemon juice, vanilla and maple extracts and beat well. Add remainder of dry ingredients mixture to creamed mixture. Then add fruit, walnuts, baking soda water and rum.

Line a bundt pan with heavy brown paper (or parchment paper) and grease well. Place a can of water in the oven while baking to keep cake moist. Bake for 4 hours.

CANberry Orange Chocolate Rounds
from Ramona

2 cups sugar, divided
2 cups raw cranberries, chopped
3½ cups flour
1 Tbsp baking powder
1 tsp baking soda
1 tsp salt

2 eggs
¼ cup vegetable oil
1 Tbsp fresh orange rind, grated
1⅓ cups orange juice
1 cup semi-sweet chocolate chips
1 cup walnuts, chopped

Preheat oven to 350°F

Grease the inside of nine 10 oz soup cans and coat with a dusting of flour. Set aside. Combine ½ cup of the sugar and the chopped cranberries and set aside. Mix the flour, remainder of sugar, baking powder, baking soda, salt. Stir well. In another bowl beat the eggs, oil, orange rind and orange juice. Add this mixture to the dry ingredients, stirring just until moistened. Once the ingredients are combined the mixture will start to rise. Do not overmix - there can still be bits of powder showing. Fold in cranberry mixture, chocolate chips and walnuts.

Divide batter into the greased cans and bake for 35-40 minutes or until they get a little golden brown on top. Remove from oven and cool for 10 minutes. Turn out the cakes onto a rack using a knife to loosen the edges but be careful that you don't cut the cakes. After cooling, wrap the individual cakes with parchment paper and foil and store overnight before slicing, or freeze for later.

these delicious cake rounds are perfect for a sweet gift or to freeze so you can grab one when company drops by.

arg!

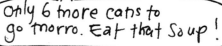

Only 6 more cans to go tnorro. Eat that soup!

Lucky Latkes
from Rick

4 potatoes, peeled and grated
1 onion, peeled and grated
1 tsp baking powder
1/3 cup flour

2 eggs
3/4 tsp salt
pepper to taste
vegetable oil for frying

Rinse the potatoes in cold water then mix them with onion, baking powder, flour, eggs, salt and pepper.

In a large skillet, pour in oil until it's about 1/8" full. When the oil is very hot, drop big spoonfuls of the latke mixture in to make pancakes. Gently flatten the latke and brown well on both sides. Absorb excess oil with a paper towel before serving the latkes.

Serve with sour cream and applesauce! Or at breakfast with onions, garlic and hot sauce, paired with eggs!

Yorkshire Pudding
from Anne

1 cup flour	pinch of salt
1 cup milk	12 tsp of oil
1 egg	

Preheat oven to 375°F

In a muffin tin, place a tsp of oil in each cup. Place in oven and heat for 30 minutes.

Mix together flour, milk, egg and salt in a bowl.

Remove muffin tin from oven and raise temperature to 400°F. Divide batter into muffin cups, filling them 2/3 full. Place in the oven for 20 minutes. The puddings should begin to rise. Turn oven back down to 375°F and cook for an additional 5 minutes or until golden. Remove and serve immediately.

Secret Stuffing
from Ramona

2 large loaves of bread, diced or ripped (it crumbles better if it's a bit dried out)	1 Tbsp ground ginger
1 large onion, diced	1 Tbsp pepper
1/3 cup parsley	1 tsp salt
1/3 cup savory	1/3 - 1/2 cup butter
1/3 cup ground sage	2-3 cups fresh cranberries
	3/4 - 1 cup low sodium stock or water

Combine all the ingredients in a large bowl and mix together – it works best with your hands! If you're using frozen bread, don't add the stock or water! You want the smells to rise up and hit you in the face, but you don't want it to look green (too much sage will turn it green!). Stuff it all directly into the bird, but don't squeeze it in too tight or it'll be clumpy after.

If you're baking it separately in a dish, add a little more butter or oil olive on top for moisture. Cover it in foil and bake it for 1 hour at 350°F. Uncover it for the last 20 minutes to give it a golden brown top.

More More More Matzah Crunch
from Francie

4-6 unsalted matzah pieces
1 cup unsalted butter
1 cup brown sugar, firmly packed
1 cup chocolate chips, chopped
1 cup slivered almonds, toasted

Preheat oven to 375°F

Line a large cookie sheet with foil or parchment paper. This is important because it gets sticky during baking. Line the bottom of cookie sheet with matzah, and use the broken pieces to fill in spaces.

In a pan or double boiler, combine butter and sugar. Cook over medium heat, stirring constantly. Remove from heat and pour over matzah. Add toasted almonds on top. Place cookie sheet in oven and reduce the heat to 350°F. Bake for about 15 minutes. Check every few minutes to make sure mixture is not burning. If it's turning brown, remove from oven, and put it back in once the temperature has lowered to 350°F. Remove from oven and sprinkle with chocolate immediately. Let stand for about 3 minutes and then spread chocolate over matzah.

While still warm, break into squares or pieces. Chill in the pan, then place in the freezer to set.

♡ A yummy traditional Jewish recipe

A Brisket A Brasket
from Miriam who got it from someone else who got it from someone else...

5 lbs brisket
1 package onion soup mix
1 tsp dry mustard powder
2 Tbsp oil

1 cup barbeque sauce
3 Tbsp honey
1/2 tsp pepper

Mix onion soup, dry mustard and oil to form a paste. If it's too dry, you can add more oil. Rub paste on both sides of the brisket then seal it in heavy duty foil. Place it in the fridge overnight.

Preheat oven to 300°F

Place the foil-sealed brisket in a roasting pan for 45 minutes per lb, or a minimum of 4 hours. While the meat is cooking, combine the barbeque sauce, honey and pepper in a glass bowl. When there is 30 minutes left, open foil and pour mixture over the roast. Continue to bake uncovered.

For easier slicing, cool in the fridge. Slice and pour the gravy back over the meat. Reheat in heavy duty foil before serving.

Did you know that briskets are cooked all over the world? This particular recipe is often served during holidays, but brisket is cooked in all different ways all over the world. You can eat it smoked, boiled, grilled, in a taco... And you can eat it in the U.S., Korea, Thailand, Britain, Canada, Mexico...

Harvest Apple Torte
from Ashley

Crust:
½ cup butter
⅓ cup sugar
½ tsp vanilla extract
1 cup flour

Filling:
8 oz cream cheese
1 egg
¼ cup sugar
½ tsp vanilla extract

Topping:
1 tsp cinnamon
¼ cup sugar
2 cups apples, sliced
¼ cup nuts, chopped

Preheat oven to 375°F

Mix all the crust ingredients together and pat them into the bottom of a 9" springform pan.

Mix all of the filling ingredients together until the cheese is fluffy and then spread over crust.

Combine cinnamon and sugar and coat the apples. Arrange the coated apples on the cheese layer. Sprinkle with nuts. Bake for 45 minutes. Let cool before removing springform.

Wondrous White Chocolate Biscotti
from Laurie

2½ cups flour
1 tsp baking powder
½ tsp salt
1½ cups sugar
½ cup butter, softened
2 large eggs
½ tsp almond extract
1½ cups dried cranberries
6 oz white chocolate, chopped
¼ cup almonds, chopped (optional)
1 egg white

Preheat oven to 350°F

In a medium bowl, combine flour, baking powder and salt. Whisk to blend. In another bowl, beat sugar, butter, eggs and almond extract until well blended. Mix in the flour mixture, then add cranberries, chocolate and almonds if desired.

Divide dough into three parts and shape into rectangular logs that are 2½" wide, 9½" long and 1" high. Flatten the tops and sides of each log. Line 2 cookie sheets with parchment paper and place no more than 2 logs on each cookie sheet.

In a small bowl, whisk egg white until foamy and glaze top and sides of logs. Bake on middle rack for about 25 minutes, or until golden brown. Remove from oven and after 5 minutes, cut logs on diagonal into ½" slices. Turn biscotti on side and discard parchment paper. Place biscotti back in oven and bake for another 10 minutes. Turn biscotti over and bake for 5 more minutes.

I Wish I Wish for a Mushroom Knish
from Frederick

Dough:
2 eggs
1/2 cup oil
1/2 cup warm water
1/2 tsp salt
2 tsp baking powder
2 1/2 cups flour

Filling:
8 potatoes, peeled and cubed
3 medium onions, chopped
1/4 cup vegetable oil
8 oz mushrooms, chopped
2 eggs, beaten
salt & pepper to taste

Preheat oven to 350°F

In a large bowl, mix eggs, oil and water together. Add in salt, baking power and flour and mix until just blended. (Don't over mix or the dough will get tough!). Let the dough stand for about 10 minutes.

To start the filling, boil the potato chunks in salted water until tender. Drain them, then place in a large saucepan over medium-high heat for about 1 minute and make sure the potatoes don't stick to the pan. Mash the potatoes together and set aside in a big bowl.

Sauté the onions in oil until golden brown, then remove from pan. Sauté the mushrooms in the onion pan, adding salt & pepper to taste. Mix the mushrooms, onions, eggs and potatoes together, and add salt & pepper to taste.

Divide the dough into four pieces and coat each one with flour. Shape into rectangles and roll out as thin you can.

Spoon a row of filling along one side of the dough, about 1" from the edge and then roll it up. With your hand, cut the rolls into 2" sections. Press the edges in and place them on one end on a lightly greased cookie sheet. Bake for 35 minutes or until golden brown.

Melt In Your Mouth Sugar Cookies
from Cynthia

Cookies:
2 eggs
1½ cups sugar
1½ cups butter
½ tsp vanilla extract
1 tsp cream of tartar
3½ cups flour
1 tsp baking soda

Icing:
1 cup unsalted butter, softened
pinch of salt
4 cups icing sugar
¼ cup whipping cream or milk
½ tsp vanilla extract

Preheat oven to 350°F

In a large bowl, beat the eggs and mix in sugar, butter, vanilla, and cream of tartar. Mix the flour and baking soda together and mix into the wet ingredients. Chill dough. Roll out and cut into your favourite shapes. Place on a greased cookie sheet and bake for 8-12 minutes.

To make icing, mix butter with salt until smooth. Mix in a third of the sugar and then half of the cream, and then repeat until all the sugar and cream are mixed in. Mix in the vanilla.

Decorate sugar cookies with icing in any way you want!

Holla for Challah
from Debbie

3 cups flour
2 Tbsp sugar
2 Tbsp fast-rising dry yeast
1 1/2 tsp salt
2 large eggs

1 cup hot water (120-130°F)
2 Tbsp vegetable oil
1 egg white (for egg wash)
2 tsp sesame seeds

In a large bowl, mix flour, sugar, yeast and salt. In a glass measuring cup filled with 1 cup of hot water, add oil, 2 whole eggs, and gently mix together. Mix the wet ingredients into the dry until well combined, adding a bit more flour if it's too sticky. Knead the dough for a couple of minutes. Let the dough rest for about 5 minutes on a floured surface.

Divide the dough into 3 equal sized balls and roll into long strips and braid into a challah. Place on a greased cookie sheet. Or for round challah style, form dough into a strip and coil it. Place into a greased 9" cake pan. Cover the challah with a tea towel and let it rise until doubled in volume, about 25 minutes.

Preheat oven to 350°F

Use a pastry brush to 'paint' egg white onto challah, and sprinkle with sesame seeds. Bake for 18-20 minutes.

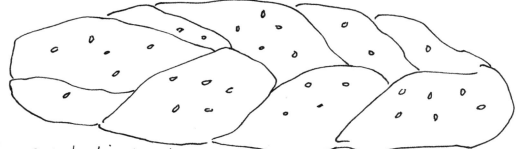

You can be 'civilized' and cut it into strips, or... you can just tear at it with your hands like we do. Yum!

When you are, like, feeling super popular, or when it's just the girls, or just the guys, or just you. That's cool too, right?

Welcome to the PARTY!

Jasp's Classic Cheese and Cracker Recipe

Opa! Greek Dip

Shrimp Dippin'

Jasp's Epic Layered Dip

Morro's Epic Layered Dip

Dashing Artichoke Dip

Artichoke Cheese Nibblies

Sweet Brie

Savoury Brie

When Olive Met Cheese Balls

Mama Castelli's Burgers

Messy Mush Burgs

Lemon Freeze

Long Weekend Lemon-Aid

'People of the World, Ice Up Your Life' Tea

Jasp's Classic Cheese and Cracker Recipe
from Jasp

1 piece of cheese
1 cracker

On a small plate, combine cheese with cracker. Make sure to place cheese on top of cracker rather than the other way around. Trust me. Add salt & pepper and pickles to taste. Let stand for 20 seconds before eating.

Serves 1

Opa! Greek Dip
from Jasp

8 oz cream cheese, softened
6 oz feta cheese
2 garlic cloves, minced
1/2 cup sour cream
1/3 cup red onion, chopped
2 Roma tomatoes, chopped
1/2 cup cucumber, chopped
1/2 cup kalamata olives, de-pitted and chopped

Mix together cheeses, garlic and sour cream then spread on a very large plate or platter. Top with red onion, then tomatoes, then cucumbers, then olives. Serve with celery sticks and soft pita triangles.

With these dips someone is sure to come to the party this time.

Shrimp Dippin'
from Jasp

1 can shrimp, well rinsed and drained
8 oz cream cheese, softened
2-4 Tbsp mayonnaise (depending on how creamy you want it!)
1/4 cup chili sauce
1/4 cup green onions, chopped

Mix together shrimp, cream cheese, mayonnaise and chili sauce until the shrimp is broken up into small pieces. The chili sauce will turn it pink and pretty! Add in the green onions and stir. Serve with rippled potato chips. Seriously. Don't even try eating it with plain chips. I'll find you. Yum!

Epic Layered Dip (The Best)
from Jasp

↳ *Yummy Version* ♡

The hit of the party!

Layer 1: The Creamy Stuff
8 oz cream cheese
½ cup sour cream
¼ cup mayonnaise
taco seasoning (as much as you like to taste)

Blend everything together and spread on the bottom of a 9x13" dish. I like to use something clear because then you can see all the pretty layers.

Layer 2: Guacamole
3 or 4 avocados
1 lime, juiced
¼ cup cilantro
¼ cup red onion, chopped
2 garlic cloves, minced
pinch of cayenne pepper
dash of paprika
salt & pepper to taste

Mash everything together with a potato masher. If you love cilantro but have a sister who thinks it tastes like soap (thanks, Morro), sprinkle it on half of the guacamole after you spread it in the dish. Make sure you taste the guacamole before you spread it on top of the creamy stuff and add more salt if you need to.

Layer 3: Salsa
1 cup of salsa

Layer 4: Black Beans
1 can black beans, rinsed and drained

Layer 5: Cheese
2 cups cheddar cheese, finely grated
(sometimes I add mozzarella too)

Layer 6: Green Peppers
1 green pepper, chopped

Layer 7: Tomatoes
2 Roma tomatoes, chopped

Layer 8: Green Onions
1 bunch green onions, chopped

Admire your dip and try not to eat it before your friends arrive. They won't be as impressed with it if it is mostly gone. Put it in the fridge to keep it out of sight so you're not tempted to eat it. Serve it with **BLUE** corn chips!

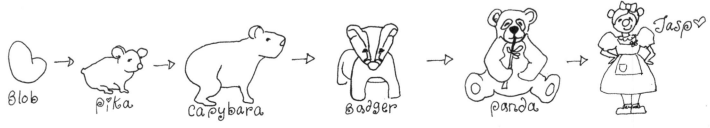

Blob → Pika → Capybara → Badger → Panda → Jasp ♡

Epic Layered Dip (Better than Jasp's)
from Morro

☆ Healthy Version ☆

Your body will thank you!

Layer 1: Beans
1 can black beans, rinsed and drained
1-2 Tbsp chili powder
1-3 tsp cayenne pepper

Layer the beans in a clear, glass dish...like a small casserole dish. Then sprinkle on the chili powder and cayenne pepper, adding lots if you like it really spicy, or just a pinch if you have a sister who doesn't like it too hot.

Layer 2: Guacamole
1 avocado
1 garlic clove, minced
squeeze of lemon
salt & pepper to taste
1 cup plain yogurt

Smash the avocado and mix in the garlic, lemon, salt & pepper. Then mix in the yogurt – 2 layers in 1!

Layer 3: Salsa Verde
5-6 medium tomatillos
1-2 hot green chilies ← like serano or jalapeno
½ small onion
2 garlic cloves
2 Tbsp fresh cilantro (optional)
dash of cumin
pinch of salt

Put the tomatillos, chilies, onion and garlic in the oven to grill for 5 minutes, flip them and grill at 350°F for another 5 minutes so they soften and start to blacken. Pop them into a blender with the spices and herbs and blend until it looks like salsa. You can add a bit of oil or water if it is too thick.

Layer 4: Pico De Gallo
2 tomatoes, diced
¼ red onion, diced
1-2 jalapeño peppers, diced
handful of cilantro or parsley
squirt of lime

Chop all the ingredients and mix 'em up! You can use cilantro if you are into that sort of thing but I prefer parsley because cilantro tastes like soap.

Layer 5: Cheeses
Grate some Canadian feta and some mozzarella or your fave old cheddar. Grate it right over the top on the small-holed grater so it looks like a light dusting of snow. Add as much or as little as you like.

Layer 6: Peppers
1 red pepper, diced

Sprinkle on top to make it pretty!

Serve with **RED** corn chips!

Variation: You can also use mixed beans and cook them with some beer for the bottom layer to make a warm dip. Pop the whole dish in the oven for a few minutes before serving - and use oven mitts!

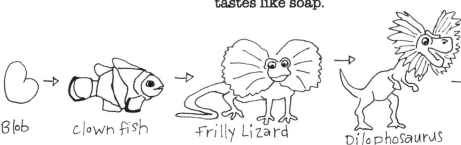

Blob → clown fish → Frilly Lizard → Dilophosaurus → Heron →

MORROA

Dashing Artichoke Dip
from Lauren

8 oz cream cheese
1 cup sour cream
1/2 package frozen spinach, thawed and drained
1 can artichokes, drained and chopped
1/3 cup mozzarella, grated
1/2 cup Monterey jack, grated
1/4 cup parmesan, grated
1 garlic clove, minced

Preheat oven to 375°F

Mix everything together and put it into an oven safe dish. Sprinkle a little bit of extra parmesan on top. Bake for 20 minutes and serve with pita chips or crackers.

Artichoke Cheese Nibblies

from Caren

1/3 cup onion, chopped
2 Tbsp oil
1 garlic clove, minced
4 eggs
1 can artichokes, drained and chopped

1/4 cup breadcrumbs
2 cups sharp cheddar cheese, grated
2 Tbsp fresh parsley, chopped
1/2 tsp salt
1/8 tsp Tabasco sauce

Preheat oven to 325°F

Sauté onions in oil for about 5 minutes, or until limp. Add minced garlic and sauté for another 2 minutes. Beat eggs with a whisk until they are frothy. Add the chopped artichokes to the eggs. Then add in the rest of the ingredients and mix together. Pour into greased mini muffin tins and bake for 30 minutes, or until firm.

guess what? Artichokes are a variety of thistle.

Sweet Brie
from Debbie

½ cup butter
1 cup demerara or dark brown sugar
½ cup pecans, chopped
½ cup raisins
1 package puff pastry

9" round block of brie
1 granny smith apple, peeled, cored and thinly sliced
1 egg, beaten (for egg wash)

Preheat oven to 350°F

In a large saucepan, melt butter and mix in sugar, pecans and raisins. Stir well.

Roll out pastry into 2 rounds large enough to enclose brie. Place 1 piece of dough on a parchment paper lined cookie sheet. Then place brie in the centre of the dough and pour the sugar mixture on top. Place apple slices over mixture, in a circular design. Finally, take the other piece of dough and place it on top. Press the upper and lower dough pieces together, fully covering everything, and making sure the 'seams' are well sealed or it will ooze. You can make flowers or designs with excess dough for decoration on top! Brush the dough with egg wash.

Bake for about 20 minutes or until the pastry is puffed. Let it sit for about 15 minutes before cutting or it will ooze too much.

YUM. YUM. yum. yum. YUM. yum. yummy. YUM.

Savoury Brie
from Cleo

9" round block of brie cheese
4 oz sundried tomatoes, chopped
3 garlic cloves, minced
2 Tbsp parsley, chopped

Preheat oven to 350°F

Mix the tomatoes and garlic together and spoon over brie in an ovenproof dish. Bake for 15 minutes, or until cheese is ooey gooey on the inside – you'll know this because when you poke the rind, it will be soft. Sprinkle with parsley to garnish. Serve with your favourite crackers and enjoy!

When Olive Met Cheese Balls
from Jasp

½ cup butter, softened
2 cups sharp cheddar cheese, grated
1 cup flour
½ tsp salt
1 tsp paprika
1 jar pimento olives, drained

In a mixing bowl, cream the butter then add cheese, flour, salt and paprika. Chill for 30 minutes in the fridge, then shape into 1 Tbsp sized dough balls wrapped around an olive. Freeze until they're firm.

Preheat oven to 400°F

Place the cheese balls on a cookie sheet and bake for 15-20 minutes. Serve to happy mouths – but wait until the balls cool for a few minutes, so the mouths stay happy and don't get burnt and sad...

Mama Castelli's Burgers
from Alex

3 lbs ground beef, uncooked
2 lbs ground pork, uncooked
1-2 eggs
½ cup parmesan, grated
½ cup ketchup or your favourite barbeque sauce
½ cup breadcrumbs
2-3 garlic cloves, minced
½ large onion, diced
salt & pepper to taste

In a large bowl, add both meats together and mix with one egg. Add the cheese, ketchup and breadcrumbs and mix again. Then stir in onions and garlic. (If the mix is a bit dry, add another egg.) Finally, add salt and pepper to taste before shaping into patties. This amount should make about 15-20 burgers.

Variation: For fun, try adding 3 Tbsp of cumin and 3 Tbsp of chili powder for taco burgers. You can even add minced jalapeños for some extra kick.

Great for the barbeque. But don't burn them :)

Messy Mush Burgs
from Morro and Jasp

2 Tbsp olive oil, divided
1 yellow onion, finely chopped
2 garlic cloves, minced
8 oz cremini mushrooms, grated
big handful fresh parsley, chopped
3/4 cup breadcrumbs
1 Tbsp tahini
1 Tbsp hoisin sauce
1/4 cup pecans, toasted and chopped
1 Tbsp soy sauce
1/2 tsp dried basil
1/2 tsp dried sage
salt & pepper to taste
1 cup quinoa, cooked (1/2 cup uncooked)
1 cup red lentils, cooked (1/2 cup uncooked)

Heat up 1 Tbsp of olive oil in a pan over medium heat and toss in the onions and garlic. Sauté them for about 5 minutes or until the onions get a little soft. In a big bowl, mix the onions and garlic with the mushrooms and parsley and toss in breadcrumbs, tahini, hoisin sauce, pecans, soy sauce, basil, sage, salt & pepper. Add in the quinoa and lentils and mix it all up together. Put your big bowl of messy mushroom mix in the fridge for half an hour-ish. Make it into patties with your hands – get messy. You just have to.

Heat up 1 Tbsp of oil in a pan, and fry the mush burgs over medium heat for about 5 minutes on each side, or until they're crispy. Mush burgs sometimes like to get unruly and fall apart – don't let them!

You can also bake your mush burg in the oven at 350°F for 15-20 minutes for a firmer texture. Eat it on a bun with all your favourite burg toppings!

Lemon Freeze
from Laurie and Debbie

Crust:
1½ cups graham cracker crumbs
4 Tbsp oil or butter, melted

Lemon Filling:
3 whole eggs
3 egg yolks
½ cup lemon juice
½ lemon, zested (optional)
1¼ cups sugar
3 egg whites, room temperature
3 Tbsp sugar

Meringue Topping:
6 egg whites, room temperature
½ cup sugar

Preheat the oven to 350°F

To make the crust, mix graham cracker crumbs with butter or oil until well blended. Press into the bottom of a greased springform pan. Bake for 7 minutes. Cool completely.

To make the filling, in a double boiler stir the eggs, yolks, lemon juice, zest, and 1¼ cups sugar. Cook until just thickened, stirring constantly. When bubbles start popping, remove from heat. Do not overcook! Cool completely, and whisk while it cools. Then in another bowl, beat the 3 egg whites until foamy. Then add 3 Tbsp sugar and beat until stiff, but not dry. Fold the egg white mixture into the lemon custard. Pour the mixture onto the crust and freeze for a minimum of 5 hours.

To make the meringue, beat 6 egg whites until foamy. Add sugar and beat until stiff and peaks form. Pour on top of frozen lemon freeze. Bake at 400°F just until golden – about 5 minutes or less. Watch carefully to make sure that it does not burn! Refreeze until ready to serve. Take out 10 minutes before serving.

Variation: Substitute lemon with lime for a different kind of delicious treat!

Long Weekend Lemon-Aid
from Morro

It helps you get the party goin' on...

2 big lemons
3 stems of mint from the garden
1-5 Tbsp honey
2 cups hot water
ice cubes

Wash the dirt and fly spit off your mint. Pour hot water over the mint and honey (start out with a little honey – you can add more later). Squeeze the lemons. Fish the seeds out of the lemon juice – you don't want those in your drink. Mix the lemon juice into the minty-honey mixture and add some more honey depending on how sweet or sour you like it. Dump in two big handfuls of ice cubes and watch them melt in the hot water. Taste it to see if it has enough of everything according to your tasty buds.

'People of the World, Ice up Your Life' Tea
from Morro

2 Tbsp of your favourite tea (green or rooibos are some good ones)
2 Tbsp agave
4-5 cups boiled hot water
ice cubes

Brew your favourite tea in hot water. Add some agave to sweeten, depending on how sweet you like it and the kind of tea. Pop it into the fridge to cool if you have lots of time, or add some ice cubes to quicken up the process. Sweet and refreshing!

Full of Love

When your heart is bursting at the seams and you want to smother the world in kisses because you just have so much darn love to give. xo

This is the Cake that Never Ends, Yes it Goes on and on, My Friends...

Pluk's Tiramisu

Ooey Gooey Love Bites

Buttery Tarts

Psst...It's Vegan Chocolate Mousse

Our Pie Filling

Our Pie Pastry

This is the Cake that Never Ends, Yes it Goes on and on, My Friends....

from Morro and Jasp

1 cup sugar
1 cup milk
1 cup flour

Mix these three ingredients and store in a container on the counter. Don't put it in the fridge. Stir this friendship mix every day for six days. On the seventh day, add:

1 cup sugar
1 cup milk
1 cup flour

If you are receiving this recipe from a friend start here.

Remove half of the friendship mix (3 cups) and set aside to give to a friend along with the copy of the recipe (it is a friendship cake after all!)

Preheat oven to 325°F

To your half of the friendship mix, add:

2/3 cup oil
3/4 cup sugar
3 eggs
2 cups flour
1/2 tsp salt
2 tsp cinnamon
2 tsp baking powder
1/2 tsp baking soda

Now, you have friendship batter! Pour half of this friendship batter in a greased 8x13" pan. Cover with 2 cups of your favourite apple pie filling. Then make this sugar mixture:

1/2 cup white sugar
1/2 cup brown sugar
1/2 cup nuts, chopped
1/2 cup oats
1/2 tsp cinnamon
1/2 cup butter, melted

Add half of this sugar mixture on top of the pie filling. Then cover with the rest of the friendship batter. Then top it with the remainder of the sugar mixture.

Bake for 90 minutes and let stand to cool before removing from pan.

Pluk's Tiramisu

from Pluk

1 cup whipping cream
1 cup mascarpone
3 Tbsp sugar (or vanilla sugar if you have it), divided
1/4 cup cocoa powder (plus more to sprinkle on top)
2 Tbsp rum
1/4 cup brewed espresso
1 package ladyfingers

Whip the cream until fluffy then stir in the mascarpone and 2 Tbsp sugar through the whipped cream and set aside.

Mix cocoa powder, 1 Tbsp sugar, rum and espresso together.

Dip the ladyfingers in the liquid mixture and place a layer of them in a medium sized glass dish. Cover with a layer of the cream mixture. Repeat layers until the dish is full, drizzling any remaining liquid on the cookies before the last layer of cream. Make sure to end with a layer of cream at the top. Sprinkle with cocoa powder. It tastes better after a night in the fridge, if you can wait that long! Otherwise, an hour or two will be fine.

I can fit 8 lady fingers in my mouth at one time. Yum.

That's our friend Pluk. →

That's our friend Pluk's rubber chicken →

Ooey Gooey Love Bites
from Morro and Jasp

14 oz caramels
3 Tbsp water
1½ cups pecans, chopped
1 cup crisp rice cereal

3 cups milk chocolate chips
1½ tsp shortening
sea salt

Unwrap the caramels and put them in a saucepan (not your mouth!) and melt them with water over low heat. Stir them and watch them get gooey. Once they're smooth, drop in the pecans and cereal and stir it all up until everything is covered in the ooey gooey caramel mixture.
Drop little love bite-sized spoonfuls onto 2 well-greased pans and chill for 10 minutes or until solid.

In a double boiler, melt chocolate chips and shortening and mix 'em up until it's all nice and smooth. Don't eat it or you'll burn your tongue (ask Morro). Dip the chilled love bites into the melty chocolate, providing them with extra love, and making sure they're totally covered in chocolate. Put them back onto the greased pans and sprinkle sea salt onto each one for another layer of love. Put the pan into the fridge until the chocolate is hard. Try not to eat them all at once. After all, they're for sharing with someone you love...

Two of our most favourite recipes to pair with pie crust.

Buttery Tarts
from Marie

¼ cup butter, softened
1 cup brown sugar, lightly packed
1 egg, beaten
2 Tbsp cream or milk
1 tsp vanilla extract
12 unbaked tart shells
Optional: ½ cup raisins, walnuts, or pecans

← Or mix 'em all together.

Preheat oven to 375°F

Cream butter and sugar together in a mixing bowl. Add egg, cream and vanilla. Beat until well blended. If you want raisins or nuts, mix them in. Pour the filling into the tart shells - they should be about ¾ full. Bake in the oven for about 20 minutes. The pastry should be light brown and the filling will be bubbly. Remove from oven and let sit for 5 minutes.

Psst...It's Vegan Chocolate Mousse
from Shelby

21 oz raw soft tofu
¾ cup chocolate, chopped (I recommend Ghirardelli dark)
sugar to taste *← We like to add ¼ cup sugar.*

Option 1: 1 ripe banana & ⅓ cup peanut butter
Option 2: A couple shakes of cayenne pepper & red chili flakes

Melt the chocolate in a double boiler. Then blend together tofu, chocolate and sugar. If you're feeling awesome, you can add a banana and peanut butter. If you're feeling spicy, you can add cayenne and chilies. Blend until smooth.

If you want to, you can pour it into a baked piecrust (see Our Pie Pastry for a good one) and let it cool and solidify for at least 4 hours in the fridge.

Eat the heck out of it.

Our Pie Filling
from Morro and Jasp

1 pint fresh local strawberries (frozen works too, but it's not as good)
3-4 stalks fresh local rhubarb (ditto)
1-3 cups sugar (it depends on how sweet you like it)

Wash and clean your strawberries. Take off the little green stem and leaf part on the strawberry – you can throw most of them in the compost bin but you have to eat at least three because they are good for you. Then slice the strawberries into thick chunky slices.

Wash and clean the rhubarb and cut it into chunks – they can be a bit chunkier than the berries. Get a big pot that has a lid. Throw in the rhubarb and pop the lid on. Let it cook on low heat while you think of a really nice memory for every finger that you have, including the thumbs (if you have thumbs). Toss in the strawberries and a bit of sugar. We like to add a bit of sugar at a time so it doesn't get too sweet.

Let them cook down a bit without the lid. If it's too dry, add the lid. If it's too wet, take off the lid – it traps in the moisture (eww...that's such an icky word...'moisture'). Cook it all for the amount of time that it takes you to think of one really nice person in your life for every toe that you have (don't feel badly if you don't have ten toes, not everyone does). Taste the fruit to see if it's sweet or sour to your liking. Morro likes it a bit sour but Jasp likes a lot of sugar, so...

Once it's at the right sweetness and the fruit is softened it's ready. It should still be chunky because it's good that way. If it is really runny (because some berries have a lot of juice) you can whisk in just a little flour or cornstarch to help thicken it but be careful because if you add too much you'll be able to taste it.

Pour your filling into a pie shell or into a jar and store it in the fridge until you are ready to use it. Stare at it for a minute while you think about who you are going to share it with.

Our Pie Pastry
from Morro and Jasp

1/3 cup butter
1/3 cup vegetable shortening
1 1/2 cups flour

2 Tbsp sugar
1/2 tsp salt (unless you're using salted butter)
4-6 Tbsp ice water

Measure and freeze the butter and shortening for at least 30 minutes. Put some water in the freezer so it gets good and cold for when you need it. It is the secret to a good pastry. Mix up your flour, sugar and salt in a big bowl. Grate in the butter and coat it with the flour mixture. Grate in the shortening and gently toss it all with your fingers – not too much but make sure there are no clumps. Use the ice water and a spatula to hold the dough together. It'll still be a little bitty, but don't handle it too much because the lumps of butter and shortening are what makes it flaky when baked. Form it into a disk shape and pop it into a plastic bag. Toss it into the freezer for an hour or so. Sometimes we prep the dough the night before in which case you can put it in the fridge not the freezer.

Preheat the oven to 350°F

Take the dough out of the fridge/freezer. Squish together the disc to reinforce its clumpness. Throw some flour around on the surface of the counter and flour your rolling pin.

For Pie:
Cut the dough into two pieces, one slightly bigger than the other (the slightly smaller one is for the lid). Roll out the dough for the bottom, making sure to keep it floured underneath so it won't stick to the counter. Put it into a pie dish and put your filling in. Roll out the lid, cutting the pi (3.14...) symbol in the middle. With your finger, rub some water around the edges of the bottom pie shell so when you put the lid on it'll help them stick together. Press the edges of the pie together with a fork or with your thumb and then trim off the extra dough with a knife to make it pretty.

Pi → π

For Tarts:
Cut the dough into 9-12 pieces depending on how big you want your tarts to be. Roll each piece into ball, remembering not to handle the dough too much – the more you touch it, the less flakey it will be once baked. Roll out the small balls making sure to keep the surface floured. Fit each flat piece of dough into a muffin cup and add filling.

Note: the baking time will depend on the pie or the tart recipe. You should look for the crust to turn golden brown and start shimmering. It usually takes us about 30 minutes.

INDEX

Appetizers:
Come and Getta Bruschetta 86
Half Pennies 160
Jasp's Classic Cheese and Cracker Recipe 184
Artichoke Cheese Nibblies 189
When Olive Met Cheese Balls 191

Dips:
Homestyle Hummus & Pita Chips 51
Shrimp Dippin' 185
Opa! Greek Dip 185
Jasp's Epic Layered Dip 186
Morro's Epic Layered Dip 187
Dashing Artichoke Dip 188

Salads:
Chick Chicky Boom Chicken Salad 42
Avocado and Mushroom Super Salad 43
Kick Butt Kale Salad 44
Pump it Up Pear and Walnut Salad 44
Halloo-Me-Name Is-Raeli Couscous Salad 45
Fiesta Chickpea Salad 46
Overnight Layered Salad 47
Tickle My Tummy Tabbouleh Salad 48
Sesame Lime Crunch Slaw 50
Cupid's Caprese Salad 84
Caes(ar) the Night Salad with Take My Breath Away Croutons 85
Super Fun Marshmallow 'Salad' 163

Soups:
Spicy Coconut Lentil Soup 116
The Pretty Soup 117
What's the Dilly Pickle Soup 118
Oodles of Noodles and Beans Soup 119
Belly Full o' Black Bean Soup 120

Stews:
Baloney Stew 28
What's Your Hurry Lamb Curry Stew 59
Drunken Mushroom Stew 122
Bengali-Style Chicken Curry 124

Chicken and Turkey:
Chick Chicky Boom Chicken Salad 42
Enchilada Lasagna Casserole Layered Goodness 123
Bengali-Style Chicken Curry 124
Turkey Lurkey Quiche 141

Lamb:
What's Your Hurry Lamb Curry Stew 59

Beef:
Baloney Stew 28
I'm Gonna Make You a Meatball You Can't Refuse 58
Bring-It-On Bulgogi 60
Captain Cabbage Rolls 63
Better Than Your Mom's Lasagna 128
A Brisket A Brasket 174
Mama Castelli's Burgers 192

Fish & Seafood:
Herb Garden Salmon 41
World's Best Lobster 67
Show Me Your (Red Thai Curry) Mussels 81
Cod au Gratin 127

Beans and Legumes:
Halloo-Me-Name Is-Raeli Couscous Salad 45
Fiesta Chickpea Salad 46
Homestyle Hummus & Pita Chips 51
What's Your Hurry Lamb Curry Stew 59
Spicy Coconut Lentil Soup 116
The Pretty Soup 117
Oodles of Noodles and Beans Soup 119
Belly Full o' Black Bean Soup 120
Chana My-Sala 125
100% Canadian Maple Baked Beaners 142
Jasp's Epic Layered Dip 186
Morro's Epic Layered Dip 187

Vegetable Dishes:
Yummiest Broccoli 40
Yummiest Brussels Sprouts 40
I-Want-Junk-But-I'm-Watching-My-Figure
Kale Chips 49
Chana My-Sala 125

Pasta and Rice Dishes:
Summery Fresh Pasta 35
Captain Cabbage Rolls 63
Rad Pad Thai 64
Zen Zucchini and Mushroom Risotto 65
Moonlight Sonata Ricotta Gnocchi 87
Tough Day Truffle Mac & Cheese 98
Tougher Day Tomato Mac & Cheese 99
Better Than Your Mom's Lasagna 128

Side Dishes
Doughboy Dumplings 122
Southern Cheese Grits 126
100% Canadian Maple Baked Beaners 142
The Infamous Green Jello Mould 'Salad' 163
Super Fun Marshmallow 'Salad' 163
Yorkshire Pudding 172
Secret Stuffing 172
I Wish I Wish For A Mushroom Knish 177

Potato Dishes:
Heal My Heart With Cheese Potatoes 103
Thrice Cooked Brekkie Taters 138
'You Say Potato, I Say Potato' Potato Egg Tart
140
Lucky Latkes 171
I Wish I Wish For A Mushroom Knish 177

Cheesy Dishes:
Spinach. Cheese. Pie. Bam. 62
Cheese Fawn-Over-You-Due 82
Cupid's Caprese Salad 84
Moonlight Sonata Ricotta Gnocchi 87
Tough Day Truffle Mac & Cheese 98
Tougher Day Tomato Mac & Cheese 99
Heal My Heart With Cheese Potatoes 103
Enchilada Lasagna Casserole Layered
Goodness 123
Southern Cheese Grits 126
Cod au Gratin 127
Better Than Your Mom's Lasagna 128
Jal & Ched Cornbread 143
Half Pennies 160
Jasp's Classic Cheese and Cracker Recipe
184
Artichoke Cheese Nibblies 189
Sweet Brie 190
Savoury Brie 190
When Olive Met Cheese Balls 191

Seasoning:
Can You Handle the Heat Jerk Seasoning 61
Mary's Mustard Relish 162

Breads, Muffins and Loaves:
Morro's Mean Lean Muffins 52
'What? I'm Eating My Veggies!' Zucchini Loaf 53
The Fruit Bread of Destiny 68
Toast 137
Jal & Ched Cornbread 143
Cinnamony Sugary Quick Bread 144
Banana-Nana Bread 155
Slow as Molasses Buns 157
Good Ol' Carrot Pineapple Muffins 161
Yorkshire Pudding 172
Holla for Challah 179

Pancakes & French Toast:
Maple Squash Pancakes 134
Chez Shea Oven Pancake 135
Apple of My Eye Pancake 136
Grilled Cheese French Toast with Butter Rum Pears 139

Cakes & Tortes:
All the Cookies n' Ice Cream Cake 33
Mighty Mabel's Rum Cake 69
Bewitching Brittle Banana Torte 70
Beet Generation Cake 74
Sassy Flourless Chocolate Cake 92
Cried My Eyes Out Chocolate Cake 100
Why'd Ya Cheat On Me Cheesecake 102
Blueberry Buckle 153
Harriet's Magical Spice Cake 154
Sweet Raspberry Cupcakes 159
Festive Fruitcake 169
CANberry Orange Chocolate Rounds 170
Harvest Apple Torte 175
This is the Cake that Never Ends, Yes it Goes on and on, My Friends... 200
Pluk's Tiramisu 202

Pies, Tarts and Crumbles:
Peachy Keen Cobbler 27
Hi Ho Ginger Pear Crumble 27
Spinach. Cheese. Pie. Bam. 62
Buttery Tarts 204
Psst...It's Vegan Chocolate Mousse 204
Our Pie Filling 205
Our Pie Pastry 206

Squares:
Na-Na-Naimo Bars 31
Juliet's Love Letters 91
Save the Date Squares 156

Cookies:
Oatmeal Chocolate Chip Cookies 26
Cookie Surprise 30
I Can't Believe They're Not Cookies 52
Pick-Me-Up Peanut Butter Cookie Dough 106
In a Ginger Snap 158
Crispy Oatmeal Cookies 158
Pat's Shortbread Cookies 158
Classical Gingerbreads 168
Wondrous White Chocolate Biscotti 176
Melt In Your Mouth Sugar Cookies 178

Sweet Bites:
Balls, Coconut Balls 90
More More More Matzah Crunch 173
Ooey Gooey Love Bites 203

Frozen Desserts:
Super Awesome Frozen Ice Cream Peanut Butter Sponge Toffee Caramel Awesomeness 32
All the Cookies n' Ice Cream Cake 33
We Be Chillin' With Fro Yo 145
Lemon Freeze 194

Icing:

Mighty Mabel's Rum Cake 69
Beet Generation Cake 74
Classy Chocolate Ganache 92
Cried My Eyes Out Chocolate Cake 100
Harriet's Magical Spice Cake 154
Sweet Raspberry Cupcakes 159
Loyal Royal Icing 168
Melt In Your Mouth Sugar Cookies 178

Chocolate:

Oatmeal Chocolate Chip Cookies 26
Cookie Surprise 30
Na-Na-Naimo Bars 31
All the Cookies n' Ice Cream Cake 33
Mighty Mabel's Rum Cake 69
Beet Generation Cake 74
Balls, Coconut Balls 90
Juliet's Love Letters 91
Sassy Flourless Chocolate Cake 92
Cried My Eyes Out Chocolate Cake 100
CANberry Orange Chocolate Rounds 170
More More More Matzah Crunch 173
Wondrous White Chocolate Biscotti 176
Ooey Gooey Love Bites 203
Psst...It's Vegan Chocolate Mousse 204

Fruit Dishes:

Hi Ho Ginger Pear Crumble 27
Peachy Keen Cobbler 27
Apple of My Eye Pancake 136
Grilled Cheese French Toast with Butter Rum Pears 139
A+ Applesauce 152
Harvest Apple Torte 175
Our Pie Filling 205

Beverages:

Dandy Brandy Red Sangria 80
White Fuzzy Peach Sangria 80
Easy Peasy Rosy Posey Sangria 80
Homemade Wine 111
Long Weekend Lemon-Aid 195
'People of the World, Ice Up Your Life' Tea 195

Vegetarian:

Most of the dishes are vegetarian or have a vegetarian option, unless they have meat in the title.

Vegan:

(Some of the following recipes list butter to grease or fry in, but it can be substituted for margarine or an oil of your choice.)
Avocado and Mushroom Super Salad 43
Fiesta Chickpea Salad 46
I-Want-Junk-But-I'm-Watching-My-Figure Kale Chips 49
Sesame Lime Crunch Slaw 50
Homestyle Hummus & Pita Chips 51
I Can't Believe They're Not Cookies 52
Can You Handle the Heat, Jerk? Seasoning 61
Zen Zucchini and Mushroom Risotto 65 (if you leave out the cheese)
Take My Breath Away Croutons 85
Spicy Coconut Lentil Soup 116
The Pretty Soup 117
Oodles of Noodles and Beans Soup 119 (if you leave out the cheese)
Belly Full o' Black Bean Soup 120
Drunken Mushroom Stew 122
Chana My-Sala 125
Toast 137
Thrice Cooked Brekkie Taters 138
100% Canadian Maple Baked Beaners 142

Mary's Mustard Relish 162
Secret Stuffing 172
Messy Mush Burgs 193
Psst...It's Vegan Chocolate Mousse 204

Other Curiosities:
Playdough...Yes Playdough! 25
Foo's Famous Krup-tooeys 29
Super Sexy Seductive Soufflé 88

Thank yous ♥

Morro and Jasp would like to thank the following people, without whom this book would not be possible. They know that people who write books always say that, but it turns out it really is true. Thank you:

Halli Villegas, Jakob Van Schaick and Tightrope Books for publishing a book written by clowns; Nathaniel G. Moore for having this wild and wonderful idea; everyone at Coach House Books for making this book a reality, especially Rick/Simon and John DeJesus for teaching us so much; Derrick Chua and Jonathan Waldman for helping us figure out all the things we didn't know (and there were lots of them!); Amy Pataki for the beautiful foreword; Jian Ghomeshi for his wonderful words; Hannah Anderson, Matthew Edison and Anusree Roy for cooking with us; Lori Burt and Mike Cooney for lending us the most beautiful kitchen to play in; Stacy-Lee Annis for your inspiration and idea for yummy fro yo; Nina Lee Aquino, Sandra LeFrançois and Cahoots Theatre for helping us produce Morro and Jasp: Go Bake Yourself; The Toronto Fringe Festival for helping us grow; Factory Theatre for being a home to us; Colin Doyle for always helping us find new opportunities; Tim Murphy, Matt Burt and Jeni Walls for the love, support and oodles of patience; Alex Nirta for always making us feel so at home in front of the camera; Lisa Plekhanova for that certain je ne sais quois; Rick Lee, Laurie Shapiro and Ramona Green for the inspiring ideas and cooking tips; Rick Annis and Linda Laviolette for always being there; everyone who submitted a recipe that didn't make it into this book (we wish we could have included them all); everyone who ever came to see Morro and Jasp: Go Bake Yourself and took a big risk by eating our pie and sharing our love.

A special thanks to grandmothers (and grandfathers) everywhere (especially ours) who know what really matters: making delicious things that truly bring people together.

Thank you to everyone who opened their hearts and recipe books to share their special secrets with us: Hannah Anderson, Isabelle Annis (née Honey), Sheena Annis, Sheila Annis, Stacy-Lee Annis, Ian Arnold, Shelby Bond, Auntie Mabel, Lori Burt, Mrs. Castelli, Caren Davis, Jessica DeAngelis, Helen Donnelly & Foo, Michéle Drouin, Matthew Edison, Miriam Fischer, Megan Murphy, Ian, Amelia & Elliot Fyfe, Mark Gibson, Marie Paule Gillies, Bernice Green (née White), Lauren Green, Martenia Green, Ramona Marie Green, Lynn Griffin, Emma Mackenzie-Hillier, Thomas Morgan Jones, Mary Jigolyk, Chef Eric Lee, Patricia Lee, Rick Lee, Susan Lee, Kathleen LeRoux & Harriet, Debbie Lipkin, Hailey Lipkin, Christina White Marschler, Heidi Collins-McCann, Alexandra Montagnese, Chef Alan Moore, Lis Munsterhjelm, Ed & Marie Murphy, Ariel Burns, Tom, Seamus & Fiona Murphy, Christine Berg, Steven, Otto & Kristy Nederveen, Elise Newman, Alex Nirta, Laura Nordin, Ashley Orris, Cynthia Orris, Peter Pasyk, Kimwun Perehinec, Don & Donna Pocock, Kevin Riordan & Heidi Pack, Vania Riz, Anusree Roy, Mrs. Roy, Laurie Shapiro, Francie Bay Smith, Chef Thess from Southern Accent, Marleen Van Os & Pluk, Jeni Walls, and Anne Wooley.

A heartfelt thanks to all the trees that are part of this book.

And thanks to you for picking up this book and taking a chance on a couple of clowns.

Now that all the cookies are a-cookin'
the cakes are a-bakin'
the soups are a-soupin'
the stews are a-simmerin'
the food is a-healin' your soul
This is the end.

This is the end, our friends.
...just of this book...
...just for now...
...there will be more adventures...
...more stories...
...more deliciousness...
...maybe even another book...

So until then
Happy everything
And if you ever feel lonely
Come and play with us
on facebook.com/morroandjasp
on twitter @morroandjasp
on youtube.com/morroandjasp
or, at home at morroandjasp.com

We will see you soon

Love,

MORRO & JASP
XOXO